KU-178-566

WRITING FOR
CHILDREN
and getting published

New Edition

Allan Frewin Jones &
Lesley Pollinger

TEACH YOURSELF BOOKS

For UK order queries: please contact Bookpoint Ltd, 130 Milton Park, Abingdon, Oxon OX14 4SB. Telephone: (44) 01235 827720. Fax: (44) 01235 400454. Lines are open from 9.00–6.00, Monday to Saturday, with a 24-hour message answering service. Email address: orders@bookpoint.co.uk

For U.S.A. order queries: please contact McGraw-Hill Customer Services, P.O. Box 545, Blacklick, OH 43004-0545, U.S.A. Telephone: 1-800-722-4726. Fax: 1-614-755-5645.

For Canada order queries: please contact McGraw-Hill Ryerson Ltd., 300 Water St, Whitby, Ontario L1N 9B6, Canada. Telephone: 905 430 5000. Fax: 905 430 5020.

Long renowned as the authoritative source for self-guided learning – with more than 30 million copies sold worldwide – the *Teach Yourself* series includes over 300 titles in the fields of languages, crafts, hobbies, business and education.

British Library Cataloguing in Publication Data
A catalogue record for this title is available from The British Library.

Library of Congress Catalog Card Number: On file

First published in UK 1996 by Hodder Headline Plc, 338 Euston Road, London, NW1 3BH.

This edition published 2002

First published in US 1997 by Contemporary Books, A Division of The McGraw-Hill Companies, 4255 West Touhy Avenue, Lincolnwood (Chicago), Illinois 60712–1975 U.S.A.

This edition published 2002

The 'Teach Yourself' name and logo are registered trade marks of Hodder & Stoughton Ltd.

Copyright © 1996, 2002 Allan Frewin Jones and Lesley Pollinger

In UK: All rights reserved. No part of this publication may be reproduced or transmitted in any form or by any means, electronic or mechanical, including photocopy, recording, or any information storage and retrieval system, without permission in writing from the publisher or under licence from the Copyright Licensing Agency Limited. Further details of such licences (for reprographic reproduction) may be obtained from the Copyright Licensing Agency Limited, of 90 Tottenham Court Road, London W1P 9HE.

In US: All rights reserved. Except as permitted under the United States Copyright Act of 1976, no part of this publication may be reproduced or distributed in any form or by any means, or stored in a database or retrieval system, without the prior written permission of Contemporary Books.

Typeset by Transet Limited, Coventry, England.
Printed in Great Britain for Hodder & Stoughton Educational, a division of Hodder Headline Plc, 338 Euston Road, London NW1 3BH by Cox & Wyman Ltd, Reading, Berkshire.

Impression number   10 9 8 7 6 5 4 3 2 1
Year   2007 2006 2005 2004 2003 2002

ACKNOWLEDGEMENTS

In the preparation of this book, we received help, support and advice from many people, including those who kindly responded to our research questionnaires. If we have forgotten to list anyone, please forgive us. With thanks to Stephen Aucutt, Ben Baglio, Laurence Bard, Tony Bradman, John and Kate Briggs, Giles Clark, Michael Coleman, Suzanne Collier, Helen Coward, Clarissa Cridland, Tom Davey, Linda Davis, Catherine Fisher, Jennifer Flannery, Jo Fletcher, Claudia Frewin, Jonathan Gabay, Raymond Goodall, Helen Hart, Philip Gross, Bethany and Crystal Hadcroft, Sue Hart, Ron Heapy, Ursula Heckel, Frances Hendry, Louise Howton, Linda Jennings, Liz Jones, Tom Keegan, Chris Kloet, Ian Johnson, Gene Kemp, Linda Kempton, Karen King, Jeanette Larson, Helen McCann, Yvonne McLachlan, John McLay, Anne McNeil, Eva Melin, Julia Moffat, Ann-Janine Murtagh, Christopher Norris, Roger Palmer, Bette Paul, Gary Paulsen, Rubin Pfeffer, Jean and Gerald Pollinger, Marion Pollinger, all the staff at Laurence Pollinger Limited, Kate Pool, Monique Postma, David Riley, Rod Ritchie, Caryn Rothwell, Ann Ruffell, Kevin Stewart, Mary Tappisier, Peggy Vance, Jean Ure, Michael Virgo, Penny Walker, Joan Ward and Sue Welford.

This book is dedicated to Iain Brown, without whose editorial input, flair, ideas, attention to detail, friendship, humour and general nagging this book would never have made the bookshelves.

Mention must also be made of the Society of Young Publishers which has brought together so many good friends.

CONTENTS

1 WRITING FOR CHILDREN: AN EASY OPTION?

Once upon a time, someone had a really brilliant idea for a story ...

Stop right there! Do you have an idea for a story buzzing around in your head at this moment? Have you written it down anywhere? If not, put this book down *immediately* and go and get your idea onto paper, personal organizer or computer. We are not joking!

Do it *now*. Story ideas can drift in through one ear and out through the other in the time it takes to sign a letter; and there is nothing more maddening than knowing you *had* a brilliant idea, and later being unable to remember what it was.

Thus, lesson one is: always have a pen and a notebook (chalk and slate, or whatever) within reach, and write down ideas as they come to you.

Okay, have you written down that idea? If so, and you are sitting comfortably, let us begin.

How to use this book

Everyone knows that today's newspaper is tomorrow's parrot cage liner. Books, by their very nature, are different. They are much more permanent and most people are brought up to treat them with care: turn the page from the top edge, not to fold down corners to mark your place and never to scribble in the margins. A lot of adults treat books as ornaments, reading them once, placing them carefully on a shelf and dusting them every now and then. *This* is not that sort of book. These days many students sit 'open book' examinations, and are taught to see their textbooks as active tools in such a situation. They are encouraged to make marginal notes and to underline or highlight potentially important sections.

This book should be treated similarly, as a study aid.

Exercise 1

Get yourself a highlighter, pen or pencil so you can mark any points in this book that you think will be useful. Identify passages with those yellow sticky notes, or be really sinful and turn down corners of pages. Add your own notes and ideas in the margins. Make this book work for you.

We will not be handing out diplomas, but by the time you have finished this book you should be in possession of a lot of practical advice and knowledge to help you polish your writing.

One point: this book is not intended for published authors; it is aimed at those of you who have been quietly creating stories for your own pleasure or to amuse children, but who have not taken that first step towards a wider audience. Or perhaps you have been thinking, 'I'd like to write for children. How do I go about it, and how do I go about getting my name in print?' Or maybe you have been toiling away, completing stories and sending them to appropriate publishers, only to have them returned with rejection letters for your pains. Perhaps you are wondering what you are doing wrong and have decided to seek advice.

Read on.

Starting with the basics

As with any textbook, it is impossible to prejudge the level of expertise of a potential reader. This book has therefore been written as a 'beginner's guide', and in the same way that a tutor book for a musical instrument shows a novice the basics, and answers questions like 'Which way up do I hold the instrument?', this book will act as a comprehensive though basic guide to the world of children's writing. Having said that, even hardened veterans of children's writing might just learn something new!

There is no right or wrong way to write for children and, as of now, there are no necessary qualifications. You do not need a BChW (Bachelor of Children's Writing), but you will need to understand some basic guidelines which, if followed, should increase your chances of being published. The idea is that, by using this book as your study aid, you will be able to achieve your aims more quickly than by the tortuous route of trial and error. In preparing this book, questionnaires were sent to a great many published authors, publishers and other professionals involved in the world of children's books. Response times varied from same-day faxes and e-mails to return-of-post letters; and no one took longer than ten days to respond. This makes one thing very obvious – people in the book business want to help new writers and are willing to share their expertise, not to mention their mistakes and failures. (It needs to be pointed out, though, that response times for submitted manuscripts will not generally be anything like so swift. Reply times can, in fact, vary from days to many months.)

The responses to the questionnaires ranged from the unprintably funny to the grimly sober. Many encouraging and useful pieces of advice will appear in italics throughout this book. We have left the authors of these gems unedited and anonymous to protect their own interests, but have included their names in the Acknowledgements.

Dear Lesley

Good luck with the book. J wishes a certain agent would send him some bestsellers so he can buy a mansion and a yacht on the Cote d'Axur [sic].

Hope this [completed questionnaire] is helpful.

Best

[US publisher]

Exploding some myths about writing for children

First the gloomy news: if you thought writing for children was an easy option, forget it! It is probably more difficult to write the text of an 800-word picture book and get it published than it is to sell an 80,000-word fiction novel for adults. These days it is tremendously difficult for a new author writing in any area to get their foot in the door, and the children's market is certainly no exception.

Superstores 'stack 'em high and sell 'em cheap', which is great if you are an established and recognized best-selling author, but which traps first-timers in the proverbial catch-22 situation: if you have not yet been published and have no track record or identifiable readership, how do you get a publisher to give you your first chance? It is the same principle that applies to job-seekers: no experience equals no job; no job equals no experience. As they say: now get out of that!

Myth 1: Writing for children is easier than writing for adults

Some people, including a number of well-known authors of books for the adult-interest market, think that writing for children may be easier than writing for adults.

Wrong!

Even famous authors of books intended for adult readers have found that their fame does not transfer easily into the children's market. Renown in one area of writing does not necessarily smooth a path into an entirely *different* area. And that is precisely what writing for children is: a different and separate writing area, *not* an easier one. It has its own difficulties and calls on special and specific skills from its practitioners.

When writing for adults, there are almost no limits to the language you can use. You can adopt whatever style takes your fancy and produce a script on literally any subject. *And* there is a very wide range of book publishers who will consider publishing your script.

However, even the most skilled authors need a couple of elements working for them to be successful. That indefinable something called *inspiration*, and that even more ethereal something called *luck*. Into this brew, add an enormous amount of persistence, and the concoction is starting to look promising.

You would hardly credit it, but some people, even those inside publishing who should know better, still view children's books as being of lesser importance than books for adults. One established writer of children's books actually had an editor come up to him and ask him when he was going to a write a 'proper' book! The following is part of an actual letter from an editor who usually works on adult-interest books, in response to the submission of a children's short story:

> *It would do you some good to make heavier demands of your art and yourself. Although you have a gift of writing both poems and fiction for children, and there is no reason why you shouldn't continue to cultivate it, I do worry that you may be clinging to those habits as a form of security.*

What a nerve! That editor should be sat down and faced with a panel of those children's writers whose work has been loved and cherished by generation after generation of young people, and asked to explain exactly why he (or she) assumes that writing for children is some sort of security blanket for those unwilling to fully explore their talent!

> *No one should look upon writing for children as a soft option. Yes, it is in many ways far simpler than writing for adults – the books are shorter, the ideas less complex – but you need a particular type of ability to do it well. An ability to become a child, to get right inside the minds of your child characters, to see through their eyes and with their experience – while at the same time, remaining your adult self, sifting and selecting as you write.*

Myth 2: The good old days of publishing

Let us take a brief look at the good old days. An editor likes your book: she feels it has something to say and that plenty of people will want to buy it. She agrees to publish it. Success! Unfortunately editors and publishing houses no longer operate in this way. The legendary leisurely lunches are a thing of the past. Literary merit and an honourable handshake no longer lead to amiable deals and speedy decisions. Business executives and accountants have moved into publishing. (If this sounds a little like Hollywood, it should: the money people have taken over the book world in the same way that they took over the movie world.) Companies have merged, staff have been rationalized and pressure applied to cut costs and increase profits. The good old days have been replaced by tough new days.

Today an editor has to convince a meeting of editorial, production and sales people that your book is going to reach its projected sales target. In such a climate it makes sense to play safe and to publish the tried and tested author, rather than to gamble on an unknown. There will always be the 'hot property' exceptions, but on the whole you need to bear in mind that in most cases *you* are going to be The Unknown.

It is said that everyone has a story to tell. The question which occupies the minds of publishers is whether that story will be of any interest to anyone outside the author's immediate circle of friends and relations.

Myth 3: Only children buy the books

Another thing you need to bear in mind is that, as with children's clothes and children's toys, the majority of children's books are *not* bought by children. They are bought by booksellers and librarians, by teachers and bulk-buying distributors. They are bought by parents and relatives or by adult collectors and dedicated followers of a particular author's work.

In other words, your book or proposed book has mainly to attract and gain the interest of an *adult* audience.

Something else to think about is that there are less children in a population than there are adults, so the children's market is obviously going to be smaller than the adult market. Are you getting the picture? Children's publishing is a very tough and competitive market.

And what if your great idea is for a picture book? Picture books are an even smaller slice of the market, and you also have to allow for a whole number of marketing rules which are out of your control, and possibly subject to a shifting social perspective way beyond your ken. Therefore, your 800-word picture book idea will have to conform to a specific set of rules, and only then will it be able to take a leap into the fiendishly competitive world of potentially publishable material.

Now for some good news! Just when you were contemplating an easier career path, a shaft of light illuminates the gloom: the children's book market is actually healthy and expanding.

The importance of children's books

No matter what sparked your interest in writing for children, it is worth pausing a moment to consider how important books are for them. When people do not learn to enjoy reading as children, their chances of picking up the joyous habit at a later age are pretty limited.

It is sometimes said that the printed word is dead, and that the computer screen has taken over. Not true! A quick glance around on a bus, train or aeroplane soon disproves that theory. People still love the portability and ease of access of a book, magazine or newspaper. You do not need to turn them on, nor do you need to insert batteries. You can read a book wherever you like: in the bath; up a tree; on a beach. It is also still far quicker to look up an unknown word in the dictionary than it is to switch on and access the right computer program (especially if you are in the bath at the time!).

How are children intended to gain access to knowledge and information if they never learn to read and write? A reasonable level of literacy is absolutely vital in life. Try playing a new computer game without understanding the accompanying written instructions, let alone make sense of the computer itself which will allegedly supplant the printed word.

How do you apply for a job without being able to fill in a lengthy application form? The ability to write goes hand in hand with the practice of reading. Whilst modern society is crying out for increased levels of literacy, these standards are not only failing to be maintained, but in many places are falling, as statistics frequently published in newspaper articles will show. The increase in text messaging and rushed e-mails is also having a detrimental effect on standard written English.

Not everyone's contribution to society can be as clear-cut as that of a doctor, a lifeboat crew member or a charity aid worker. A children's author may never know how much joy, understanding and information his/her work has given to children all over the world, and in every situation. If your writing cheers one single child, if it provides escapism for a short time from some harsh reality, or if it teaches one new word or comprehension of a problem, then that is a significant contribution to have made.

Books are essential for children and have an important and significant role to play. There is no better medium for firing the imagination. Humans need the skills of literacy and communication – more than ever before. A significant part of that learning and literacy process will involve books.

Words of encouragement

Remember the questionnaires we mentioned earlier? Among those we canvassed were prizewinners and full-time professional authors; and one of the questions we posed concerned the most useful piece of advice given to them when they were starting out on their writing career. Their answers make for interesting reading:

> *Your readers will only read this <u>once</u>. You've got to get them first time.*

> *Keep trying, don't give up in the face of innumerable rejection slips. If you really believe in yourself you will eventually succeed.*

> *Find a gap in the market.*

> *Learn to cope with rejection. To be yourself. To write what you want to write, and strive to find your own voice, not a pale imitation of somebody else's. Write the sort of material you enjoy reading, and ask yourself if you would read with pleasure the book you have just written!*

Some considerations

In our experience, a general rule is that it takes an author about *eight years* to go from publication of a first work to the point where a living wage can be earned. The exception would be for someone producing an instant worldwide bestseller. Of course, if you do not need to go out and earn a living, then you might be able to carve a few years off the end of this timescale, but that is all! It is still a lengthy process.

The average author has to *love* writing; it is pointless going into the writing business with expectations that truck-loads of cash will shortly be rolling up to your door. It simply does not work like that.

You will need huge amounts of patience and vast quantities of perseverance. Those who devote all their time to writing will also point out that it is essentially a very *lonely* occupation.

If you have a job, keep it: you will need the money. If you are totally dedicated to writing for a living, explore the possibilities of job-sharing or part-time work, so that you can be sure of a regular and reliable income. Writing, like many freelance occupations, can be a case of swings and roundabouts, feast and famine. Gradually an author will accrue income from royalties, advances and so on, which will help through the lean times – but there is no substitute for the security of a separate safe salary. Think of that salary before handing in your resignation.

Besides needing some other source of income, you will also need to get out into the real world to keep the creative juices flowing, and to keep a balanced view of *life*. Working with other people, meeting new faces, experiencing novel or unusual situations and listening to the experiences of others will give endless fuel to your imagination. As one author says:

> *Your own experiences, and those of people around you, are a good source of ideas. I find that early writings have more resonance if they are based on something you already know. Always keep your eyes and ears open. Observe how people behave, and listen to what they say. If you want your books to be peopled with real characters, you need to become something of an expert on human behaviour.*

Exercise 2

With luck, you are already filled to bursting-point with ideas for stories, and you are only reading this book in order to learn how best to present them. But wait a minute. You may discover that your brilliantly original idea has already been done. Or the morning may dawn when you stare blankly at a blank sheet of paper or a blank computer screen with the blank feeling that the creative part of your brain will never wake up again.

Writers are always unconsciously looking around for ideas – if you know what to look for. Anything at all potentially interesting should be filed away in your memory, or preferably in a notebook (which you keep meaning to put back in your handbag since you used it last week as a telephone message pad etc.). It is seldom much use on its own: you usually need two or three ideas to gel together before you even get the glimmerings of a plot.

So, if you do not have one already, you will need a small notebook and pen. Take it everywhere with you and get into the habit of being an 'ideas detective'. Look, listen and learn from everything that is going on around you. Make especial use of any contact with real children and of things to be found in a child's world. Watch children's television programmes, browse websites aimed at children and young people, visit toy shops, take slow meanders around a shopping centre at the weekend or during school holidays, and even dare to board buses at school finishing time.

Snippets of conversation overheard in queues, fast-food restaurants or on railway platforms will no doubt open your eyes. Train yourself to observe the differences in behaviour between children. Do boys behave differently from girls? If so, in what ways? And why? Jot down ideas in your notebook, whether they come from an immediate experience or from the recesses of your own memory; the most incongruous ideas can later blossom into extraordinary storylines or a non-fiction idea.

I get my ideas from books, places, TV, from myths and legends and from using archetypal storylines. I have a notebook, nothing else.

Alongside your notebook, you should start a scrapbook. A cuttings file which will become your 'Ideas File'. A large envelope would do the job, an empty drawer, or you could go crazy and set up an alphabetical or cross-referenced subject filing system. Into your chosen system you can put newspaper or magazine clippings – eye-catching headlines or entire articles, pictures of people, buildings, scenery, cartoons, work by an inspirational artist – anything, in fact, which you think might be a future source of work.

> *For character ideas, I cut out photos from magazines/ papers/catalogues. I make a pinboard for each book, with notes beside pictures for age, character, links with others, etc.*

Later in this book we will start suggesting uses for your Ideas File, so it is best to start gathering material now. The larger your collection, the more useful it will become. Think about it: a picture in today's newspaper of a child being rescued from a burning building may be the kernel from which a whole book could grow; an article about curriculum changes in education may be the seed for a non-fiction work; a face in a magazine may awaken in you the entire personality of a central character for a book.

As we said right at the beginning, if an idea comes to you, *note it down while it is still fresh in your mind.* Then put it somewhere safe! The back pocket of a pair of jeans that are heading for the wash is *not* a good place. File it away in your Ideas File.

> *For many years I have kept an 'Ideas Folder'. Whenever an idea comes to me, even if only a snippet, or a funny or intriguing remark I have heard someone say in the street, I immediately put it in my folder. Ideas can linger therein for years before finally being put to good use.*

2 | A PROFESSIONAL APPROACH

The gulf between writing for pleasure and writing for publication is a deep and wide one. Nonetheless, it is a bridgeable one, at least with the right information and the right approach. As with any profession, a great deal of groundwork has to be done before you should attempt to assail the walls of your chosen publication house.

In this chapter we are going to look at the sort of research work you should consider undertaking before you even pick up your pen or approach your keyboard. It will not be necessary for you to try everything mentioned here, but it is important for you to *know* about them. The more you know of your intended market, the better your chances of getting your foot through the appropriate door and keeping it there.

Research

The main problem that many aspiring authors need to overcome is a total lack of *research*. It is impossible to overstress the importance of research, as every publisher would agree.

> *My advice is to read a lot of children's books, and visit many children's bookshops. Too many would-be writers have no idea what's in the marketplace or what may appeal to their readers.*
>
> *[Swedish publisher]*

The importance of research

We expect you are starting to become twitchy: after all, you are reading this book because you would like to write in a more professional way. You are probably asking yourself when does the *writing* start? Well, not just yet!

First you need to take a long, hard look at the market for your work. If you were designing a new invention, you would want to look at the opposition and conduct some market research first, would you not?

Say you have invented the multi-purpose wine-drinker's companion, a handy little device which, at the press of a button, will open a wine bottle and send it trundling around the table to fill your guests' glasses to perfection. Your enquiries would include checking patent registers to find out if your idea is unique. Then you would assess the viability of mass production, materials, branding, advertising and market potential, as well as identifying possible interested manufacturers. Finally, you would work out the most professional way to demonstrate your invention, and to whom it should be presented.

Similarly, if you went to a job interview, you would create a favourable impression by showing that you had done some homework on the employer's company.

Creating a piece of work for children and presenting it to a potential publisher is no different. The authors responding to our questionnaire said:

> *The most useful piece of advice anyone gave me was 'Go to the library and see what sort of books other people write. This will give you an idea of what publishers want.' I've no idea who said this to me, but it made me look at writing from the saleability point of view.*

> *Be aware of what is being published and keep reading modern children's fiction. Some of it will be the sort of stuff that you want to write; concentrate especially on that. And then keep writing. And promise yourself not to read any of the depressing articles about the state of publishing!*

> *Research, read and target your market.*

> *If you want to get published, then you have to write something publishers are looking for. Find out what is selling (or even better – what is going to sell next year) and then write something which will fit the bill.*

As well as researching the market, research the publishers. Not all publishers publish children's books. Not all children's book publishers publish non-fiction books. Teenage magazine publishers do not necessarily publish magazines for the pre-school age group. It is a waste of everyone's time to submit a project to an inappropriate publisher. A little research will tell you where your work is most likely to find an appreciative home, and even if you are not successful straight away, at least you will be heading in the right direction.

Where to start researching

Book places: bookshops, libraries, retailers and the internet.

The first place to start your research could be your local bookshop or library. After that, visit every bookshop and library you come across. Widen your area of research as far as is practicable. If you are away from home, check out any 'book places' you may happen across. There are a few specialist children's bookshops, but it is a good idea to root around in regular bookshops, too, and look at all other retail outlets where children's books are being sold.

Children's books are sold in all manner of places, from newsagents to service stations, from supermarkets to market stalls, from garden centres to mail-order clubs and leaflets, from television shopping channels to 'clicks-and-mortar' (and online) booksellers, from toy shops to school book fairs and clubs. Some publishers sell enormous quantities of stock through home and place-of-work sales via 'book parties', in much the same way as 'party-plan' and direct marketing operates.

Bargain and remainder bookshops are worth investigating, too. They will give you an idea of books which have not sold well, and which are being sold cheaply. There are publishers who produce glossy-but-cheap books specifically aimed at this market, and some titles may have been bought in as 'damaged stock' – these could well be bestsellers. Take the time to browse and observe.

Treat all your research visits as a real learning process. Unless you have already chosen a specific area of writing, look at *everything*. It will help you understand the market.

Cheap books – not good sellers?

As far as libraries are concerned, spending cuts have necessitated some unpredictable opening hours, particularly of specialist children's sections. You will also notice that libraries stock far fewer hardback titles and more paperbacks these days. Indeed, many children's publishers do not now produce original fiction in hardback at all. Some hardbacks have been replaced with what are called 'trade paperbacks'; these books are aimed primarily at the schools and library markets. Trade paperbacks are generally the same size as a hardback, but because of the 'soft' cover are less expensive both to produce and to buy. As libraries find their budgets cut back, they purchase more paperbacks. The problem here is that as paperbacks have a shorter lifespan than hardbacks, a popular book could vanish from the shelves when a library budget runs out and a replacement cannot be purchased.

During your research, if you are lucky enough to encounter a specialist children's librarian, you should talk to them. These people are very widely read and knowledgeable in their field. Pick an appropriate time to approach them, or arrange to go back and speak with them at a more convenient time. You never know, a good library and its staff could prove a gold mine of reference and research if approached in the right way. Also look out for information leaflets, recommended reading lists, competitions and children's events run by your library or visiting library. One author said this:

> *A children's writer's best friend is her librarian – cultivate the local children's library or department, useful for research/publicity/contacts/sales.*

The big picture

While you are researching, whether it be in libraries or bookshops, ask yourself some questions:

- Where is the children's section located?
- Is there easy access for prams and buggies?
- Is it accessible for people with disabilities?
- Is there a play area, or somewhere for children to sit and look at books?
- Are the young adult (teenage) books in a different area?

■ Can children reach books placed on the higher shelves?

■ Does the shop have a monthly magazine or guide to new/popular titles?

■ Are there online information points?

■ Are books displayed alphabetically by author?

This last question is of particular interest. Look at the shelf displays and see where you own surname would place you. You might well discover that particular letters seem very popular. This is not an accident – it is marketing! Publishers want their own books to be at eye level. If your surname begins with A you might be out of reach; if it begins with Z it might be tucked away in a bottom corner somewhere.

■ Are the books in fiction and non-fiction sections?

■ Are the books grouped in age ranges?

■ Are the books displayed face-out, or with only the spine showing?

Think of a book you know and see how easy it is to locate. Make notes of what you discover – or fail to discover. Should the staff ask pointedly if you need any help, just tell them that you are an author conducting research. You never know, you might encounter someone with both the time and the knowledge to be a help to you. For example, they may be able to tell you what their best-selling titles are. Many bookshops that are part of a group or chain have central buyers who make the purchasing decisions for the whole group; however, if you come across a person who actually buys the books for the store, you could ask them about their favourites. Ask them what titles or subjects customers request but which are not stocked or are not available.

You may discover that customers are looking for books on coping with examination stress at school. Are there such books? If so, what form do they take? What age range are they intended for? Where are they located in the shop? If there are no such books, you may have just discovered every author's potential crock of gold: a gap in the market!

You may find that the library or bookstore has a specialist who does not work on Saturdays – when most children come in. Ask yourself what that says about the priorities for *that* particular establishment. Look again at where the children's section is located, or even if there is a children's section – and then ask yourself the same question again.

Information databases

Most bookshops and libraries will have microfiche, online facilities and/or computer databases with details of an author's or publisher's entire output, as well as all titles in print and those presently unavailable or now out of print. Information on books in print is also available in regularly updated catalogues. Books are accessible on the World Wide Web: in addition to being able to browse and order books for delivery, you can now also read and download titles onto your e-book reader or personal organizer. Many publishers have their own websites. An enormous wealth of information is online. You can gather information on anything from the history of books to advertisements for the latest titles. If you are not connected to the internet, you could visit an internet café (with the added bonus of being able to eavesdrop on young people's conversations and observe their behaviour).

It is important that you make yourself aware of the variety of available information resources. You can even use them to discover if the title of your intended book has already been used. Should you decide to write under a pseudonym (a name other than your own), you will be able to find out if there are any other 'Sue d'Onyms' out there in the published world.

Choose an area to study

If by now you have chosen a particular area to study, take a good look at books in that field. Do not forget to make notes of what you see. How many pages long are the books? How large is the typeface, and what style is it? Roughly calculate the average text length of the books and note the differing needs of different age groups. Do the books have illustrations? Are they in colour or black and white? Full page or amongst the text? Are there a lot of titles by the same author? Do the books form part of a series?

You will come across a lot of books that form part of a series, identifiable by their series titles or visual style. Some series may be about one set of characters, by the same author, or under one author's name; others may be horror or non-fiction series with different authors, but sharing the same jacket logo, name and style. Series aimed at younger readers may have colour-coded or numbered recommended reading age guidelines.

Calculating the length of a book or printed manuscript

Count the number of words in ten average-length lines of print. Divide the total by ten to give an average number of words per line.

Look at several pages of text and note the average number of lines per page. Multiply the average number of words per line by the average number of lines per page. This will give you a rough idea as to the number of words per page.

Multiply this figure by the number of pages in the book. You now have a good working idea of how many words there are in the entire book.

Example: 10 words per line × 25 lines per page × 100 pages in a book = a 25,000-word text.

Make some allowance in your total figure for illustrations, chapter openings and where chapters end part-way down the page and so on.

Research on your doorstep

There could be many reasons why you may not be able to visit libraries and bookshops as often as you might wish. To compensate, you may wish to investigate the many mail-order book clubs for children which exist. Book clubs often advertise in newspaper magazines and their leaflets frequently fall out the moment they are opened!

Some book clubs require a certain purchase commitment which you may wish to think about, and the advertised prices in the catalogues (although usually lower than those in any bookshop) are unlikely to include an amount for postage and packing. Any books or audio tapes that you do order are likely to be invaluable for your research, and the regular book club catalogues will give you a good idea of current popular titles, including design fashions and prices. Do not forget to keep your receipts or invoices for purchases made in connection with your writing business, as these expenses may be offset against tax (see the section, 'Tax and accounts', in Chapter 12).

There are now dozens of websites dedicated to children's interests, books, reviews, literacy, activities, education and so on. However, if you were to enter 'children's books' into a search engine, you would have to wade through one million results!

How to search the Internet effectively

- How to search the internet effectively
- Use several search engines regularly (ask friends for recommendations), such as Google and Altavista: this will help you get to know what their strengths and weaknesses are. Use web directories such as Yahoo, when you are searching for general concepts or organizations.
- Always enter search queries in lower case. If you enter a query in upper case, or in upper and lower case, the search engine will then only return web pages that match your query exactly.
- Use quotes when searching for a particular phrase; for example, 'children's books and toys'.
- Think laterally about your query: do not just enter 'children's books' and expect to see a small number of relevant pages. Add extra search terms; for example, 'children's books' +non-fiction +UK, to exclude websites that are pertinent only to Australia or India.
- Read the search engine help pages. They are an invaluable guide to any extra features a search engine offers.
- Do not feel you have to look through all the search results returned. Often you will find a site within the first couple of pages.

■ Try entering the phrase for which you are searching as a web address. For example, if you were looking for a site that was about writing books for young people, try entering 'www.writingforchildren.com'; sometimes you might strike it lucky!

■ Look at the links pages on related sites. For example, www.open.gov.uk would offer a set of relevant links for anyone looking for further information on children's education.

There are also various magazines aimed at teachers, parents and buyers of children's books. You may consider these worth subscribing to as they contain author interviews, reviews, news of awards and event details. The reviews, for example, cover a vast array of subject matter and, amongst other things, may prevent you embarking on a project which someone else has just had published!

Other trends to keep an eye on include those in toys, merchandising, clothing, film and the media. Beware: one thing you do not want to happen is for your book to deal with something that is all the rage *now* but which will be out of date by the time your book hits the shelves. Contemporary writing needs to be able to survive short-lived fashions and to avoid becoming rapidly dated. In other words, follow the latest trends, but do not be mesmerized by them. It can take a couple of years for a book to reach publication. Micro-scooters and merchantable character crazes may reach epidemic proportions every Christmas, but in two years' time a book devoted to the craze is likely to be as unsaleable as new fads are promoted. Keep attuned to what is happening in the marketplace and, if possible, think of what might be coming next.

Good sources of information if you are thinking of writing non-fiction or entering the educational market are educational periodicals. Such publications discuss issues and trends in education, as well as containing reviews and details of educational websites. Some newspapers review children's books and materials, and have the occasional children's book supplements. Many people agree that children's books receive shamefully poor coverage from the national press and media.

Radio, television and the magazine market can keep you fairly well informed. Listen to and watch children's and teen-based programmes, as well as broadcasts for schools (often shown during the day). You should be interested particularly in book reviews, readings from books, and dramatized shows on terrestrial, digital, cable and satellite television. If you have a video recorder, set it to record programmes so that you can watch them at a time which is convenient for you.

> *I have a lot of contact with children through family, friends and regular visits to schools. I find it enormously important to keep a feel for the way children talk and behave and think ... and also to know a little about current trends and interests. Watching television is particularly useful.*

Buy a variety of children's and teen magazines on a fairly regular basis. Look at the letters pages and features. If you are not familiar with today's teen magazines, you will probably be surprised or even shocked by the topics covered!

Exercise 3

We realize that the weight of all this research is making you itch, so we suggest you pause and try this exercise for your imagination.

Take a dictionary or open a website and choose three words at random. For instance you may have selected 'nuts', 'dither' and 'steamroller'. (You may need to be a little selective with the words chosen, as we are writing for children!)

Now write a paragraph-length synopsis of a story linking the three words. Or you could try a very short story, or even a poem or limerick incorporating your three words.

Seems silly? Certainly! The sillier the words are, the better.

This technique of randomly selecting words, be it with a dictionary or from blindly poking a finger at a newspaper or book, can also oil the pistons of a seized-up imagination.

(Those more interested in writing non-fiction can use an encyclopaedia, CD-ROM or Website in place of a dictionary or book. Randomly select a heading and write down all you know on that subject, even if very little, before comparing your piece with the entry. If you select three headings, stimulate the brain cells by seeing if you can form a connection, however tenuous the link!)

Contact with children

Some authors claim to have very little contact with children, yet are still able to produce marvellous work time and time again. They are able to remember their own feelings and experiences and access their 'inner child' to create works which are avidly read and which garner ecstatic reviews. These authors clearly recollect what it is like to be a child, and how children think and comprehend the world around them.

> *I think contact with children can be overrated. The important thing is to remember what it was like to be a child. Their environment may be very different from yours, but their emotions aren't. Children still laugh at the same things you did and cry for the same reasons.*
>
> *I have little direct contact with children other than visiting schools to do book talks. I don't actually know any children and have thus come to conclude that it is not important. More important is to be flexible in your thoughts, keep abreast of modern trends and perhaps above all to go back and become as a child.*
>
> *I teach in a primary school and see children a lot. It is important, especially if you're used to reading aloud to them, so that you know how they respond to books. Having said that, I don't think about the reader much at all when I write, being so caught up with the story and satisfying myself! But the knowledge of probable responses must be there deep down.*

What of the publishers of children's books and their staff? You may be surprised at how little contact many of them have had with children since they themselves left school. Many young people work in editorial, production and marketing positions, and do not always have families of their own, so their recent experience of children can be very limited. Some enlightened publishers do send staff into schools on a regular basis and use this to get feedback on potential projects. However, an editor's possible lack of child contact should be borne in mind when working with a publisher, or coping with rejection letters.

You may be one of those people who seem to have a sixth sense for what will appeal to both children and publishers but, on the whole, successful children's authors whom we contacted felt that it is very important to keep in regular contact with children and their world.

> *I need to stay in touch with children. Language, tastes and outlook change all the time.*

> *Have as much contact as you can stand!*

> *How do you know what children like to read if you don't have contact?*

You may have children of your own, in which case you can use them as a starting point. Do not be beguiled into thinking that a bedtime story which proves a roaring success will necessarily interest an outside audience. Most children love to be read to, and simply enjoy the attention and experience. A young child might well be perfectly happy to have an attentive parent's lulling voice intoning names from a telephone directory prior to lights out!

> *My elder two children always said, 'I loved that book, Mum. You're really good.' The youngest is more critical. I like the first reaction best!*

Children's schools and interests

The friends, hobbies, schooling and interests of your own children can be very useful. Authors with children (and grandchildren) will already know what clothes, books and toys are appealing, as well as what films and television programmes are popular. They will also know what is 'in' and what is definitely 'out'.

Your social situation will narrow your field of experience. Unless you have lived with and worked amidst a broad cross-section of society, you are almost bound to have a limited understanding of other lifestyles. Therefore, it makes sense to write about situations you understand rather than experimenting with those you have never encountered. The former will always ring truer to the reader. For example, if you have daily contact with pre-school children but seldom encounter young adults, it may be a mistake to try to write realistically on teenage subjects. The language and attitudes of young adults change rapidly. Finding out what they read and watch will broaden your experience.

Sadly I don't have much contact with children, very *important from the view of listening to speech patterns and current colloquialisms.*

Your own children may have grown up and there are no grandchildren to hand. In this situation, it may be hard to remember the language and abilities of a toddler. A good parenting book will provide the answers. For example, say your story idea concerns the activities of a naughty 12-month-old baby: such a parenting book will remind you that some babies are talking at this age whilst others are not, and some are walking when others are still zipping about on the fastest knees in town.

If your children are of school age, then it is relatively easy for you to join in and meet other children from a wide range of backgrounds. Most schools and playgroups welcome parental assistance. An hour or two when you get the chance will provide you with a great deal of information. You could choose to listen to children reading, and will discover the enormous range of reading and language abilities. You will find out about favourite books and topics, humour and concerns, as well as getting an insight into your local education system. You will learn the way children are taught to read, and the reading schemes and methods used. If the non-fiction area interests you, then it may be possible to help or work as a classroom assistant on project work. This will help you to understand the educational curriculum requirements, the texts children presently work from and their ability to tackle practical work. You will also find that teachers are a valuable source of information and opinion.

I think contact with children is vitally important. I have my own, plus the children I meet at the school book club I run.

Some schools may welcome help from you even if you are not a parent, but they will ask for references to reassure themselves. If you have no children and are unable to get to a school during working hours, then there are plenty of other organizations which would welcome your involvement. These range from your local church youth group, or differently abled organizations to outdoor activity movements or first-aid organizations. A few hours on a regular basis may give you all the feedback and inspiration you require for your writing.

Should you be interested in the young adult market, then an educational course could provide the answer. Attending a school or college-run course in a subject which teenagers are taking or retaking will give you very interesting company. You could be learning keyboarding skills or how to use graphics software whilst gaining an insight into modern study methods and the social behaviour of young people.

In the previous chapter, we mentioned the importance of becoming an ideas detective. Watch, listen and learn when you are out and about and ideas will come to you, as the following author discovered:

> *I was stuck on a story about goats! Two months later I was walking past a bus stop where a gang of aggressive looking bikers in full leathers was standing. I was a bit nervous, and could see plenty of things dangling from the belt of the ugliest one who had a brass studded leather cap. As I tiptoed past, I heard Studded-Cap say: 'Yeah, I was scared to cut my budgie's toenails in case I hurt his feet, so I took him to the vet. It doesn't cost much ...' I realized that the things dangling from his belt were a pair of nail clippers and a bottle opener, not knuckle dusters. A biker with a heart of budgie feathers brought my story to a riotous conclusion.*

Listen to young people, but try not to choke in horror at some of the subjects they cover or the language they use. Nonetheless, if you produce a book filled with the same undiluted street-talk, you will discover that despite wanting realism, publishers have their limits, and the sort of language that could strip paint off a battleship, real as it may be, is unlikely to find favour. We know this sort of

NO BAD LANGUAGE

language occurs in life, but the adult book buyers may not necessarily want to condone it in print.

Conferences, societies and book fairs

There are many societies and organized events which you will find useful. Details can be found in the weekly book trade magazines, writer's reference books, libraries and so on. You will be able to subscribe to most of these societies (although some will require that you have had at least one book published). Your membership will usually bring you regular mailings of information about the world of publishing as well as the latest developments, conferences, lectures and services.

Many lectures and talks will be free to members, and not too expensive for non-members, and some conferences can be very good value. Not only will you learn a lot, but you will get the opportunity to meet other people with the same interests, and also those working in the publishing industry. Some conferences organized by professional bodies can prove very expensive; these might include, for instance, conferences on technology developments and intellectual property rights in the electronic publishing world. Fairly esoteric stuff for the beginner, and you should think carefully before committing a lot of money to such an event. Consider whether the outlay will be justified by the potentially useful information or contacts gained.

Book fairs or educational/game/computer fairs can prove invaluable research venues. You will see the latest trends and developments in the publishing and related industries. You will discover who are the biggest companies and the breadth of their product ranges – and you will get a look at the sometimes daunting competition. You might find that your latest brainwave is already on the production schedules of half a dozen other companies. Or you may spot a gap in the market. Whatever you find, there is no need to be intimidated by the sheer range and quantity. All you need to know is that the majority of material is of a very high standard, and has been thoroughly researched as a saleable commodity before it was put into production. These fairs will teach you that publishing is big business.

You need to understand exactly what is going on at a trade fair or exhibition. Basically, the exhibitors are selling their products to each other, not to the general public. They could be selling books, CD-ROMs, e-books or online content to distributors and retailers, or 'rights' (paid permission for translating a book, or any other selling area different from the original printed work) to the home or overseas markets. In any event, your presence, whilst encouraged as a potential individual customer, is not always entirely welcomed by busy sales people working under great pressure and within strict time limits. Try to take everything in whilst keeping a reasonably low profile.

The Bologna Children's Book Fair is the largest of all specialist children's book fairs and has been held in northern Italy in April for over 30 years. About 1,500 exhibitors and 3,500 publishing employees attend from over 70 countries.

Other trade professionals who attend Bologna include authors' and illustrators' agents, senior book buyers for major selling chains and book clubs, printers, designers, card, film and television producers, poster and multimedia manufacturers, all looking to buy or sell rights, or to view forthcoming products. Every hotel and flight is booked solid by the publishing trade from one year to the next and there is a tendency for prices to treble during the week of the fair.

In other words, this fair may not be the best place for a budding author to visit.

A similar story can be told of the Frankfurt Book Fair which takes place in Germany every October. Here, the entire range of book and related product manufacturers meet for the same purpose. The fair in Frankfurt is truly frantic and frenetic!

It may well be worth attending a national event such as the London Book Fair, which is held annually in March, especially if it is within travelling distance and your budget.

Some dos and dont's when attending fairs and exhibitions

■ Book fairs will be advertised in the trade magazines: do try to get tickets in advance by contacting the exhibition organizer. They can be free or cheaper if obtained prior to the commencement of the fair. Large fairs may also organize discounted travel, accommodation and entrance packages if you live too far away for a day visit.

■ Do wear very comfortable shoes.

■ Do take a bag or rucksack to carry home all the free catalogues and information exhibitors give away. Be selective about what you take – if you are not, you could end up crawling out on all fours under a mountain of paper. At the end of the last day, some exhibitors sell off display material at bargain prices.

■ Do look, listen and learn. Note potential publishers for your work. If possible, go with an interested companion, so you can discuss what you see.

■ Do not interrupt staff who are obviously in the middle of a business meeting.

■ Do not try to sell your work to anyone. The chances are that you will be speaking to the wrong people anyway and, in any event, 'cold-calling' at an exhibition is considered unprofessional and could make you very unpopular.

■ Do not be intimidated by the seemingly crowded nature of the market. Publishers are always on the lookout for new talent with innovative ideas.

Publishers' pet hates

We asked publishers what they hated most about the unsolicited submissions they receive. The replies were universally similar. Read and remember!

I never want to see another project based on talking vegetables and/or traffic cones!

[UK publisher]

I get spots and itches when I see the umpteenth little animal hopping around the forest, having small-talk with another non-interesting character. But scripts that don't even have a subject make me scream.

[French publisher]

The most ridiculous stories we receive usually involve the animation of inanimate objects (characters generally have alliterative names): Elmer the Elevator whose day has its ups and downs; Bertha the Bathtub who is worried about her bathtub ring; or the chocolate bar who runs down the street and melts on the sidewalk.

[US publisher]

A story starting with breakfast in the summer holidays. Elves, pixies and fairies. Things like Cuthbert the Cucumber, Larry Lighthouse, Freddy Foghorn, Oscar Ozone – all actual examples I'm afraid.

[UK publisher]

Eighty per cent of beginner authors in Germany write about a little raindrop, a spider or an ant. I really don't know why ...

[German publisher]

You have been warned! No twee stories. No old-fashioned stuff. And you can roll up that Teddy the Table-lamp manuscript and use it as a firelighter.

Exercise 4

For the next chapter you will need a sample of your writing. ('At last', you may say.) We are not concerned with style or content just yet, so if you do not have something obvious to hand, then a letter to a friend or a diary of your day will do, or your comments on a book you have read recently, or even your opinion on a news item. It does not matter what the subject is: just aim to write or type about two pages of A4 paper (approximately 210 mm × 300 mm).

3 | GETTING STARTED: THE TOOLS OF THE TRADE

Conveying the message

You have an idea. It could be for a picture book. It could be for a storybook. It could be for a full-length book. It could even be for a series. It could be fiction or it might be non-fiction or educational.

The question you are now asking is 'How do I get this idea out in the open?' You can tell your family and friends. You can even telephone or e-mail around the globe to let a few individuals in distant places know about it. However, if you want to get your idea across to all those people out there who might potentially find it interesting, entertaining or educational, then you have got to write it down.

Although the first item of equipment you need is a pencil and a notebook (or personal organizer or computer), before you kick-start your brain and send your pencil scurrying across the paper, or your fingers flitting over the keyboard, you need a good grasp of the language in which you will be writing.

You will probably be writing in the same language as the prospective publisher of your work. (Occasionally a book is first released by a foreign publisher in another language.) Later on we will be looking at the way in which different writing areas require differing tones, styles and contents, but right now you need to address the level of your own language skills.

Language skills

Are you writing in a language that is not your native tongue? There may be areas in which you are going to need help. There may be educational, parenting, social or ability reasons why your language is not as skilled, nor your command of words as extensive as you would like it to be. You are going to be writing in words, phrases and sentences that must convey your message to a wide variety of people, all of whom need to understand what you are trying to say.

Language works on many levels. It ranges from *eloquent* to *slang*, from ancient to modern. Language is in a constant state of flux, with old words falling out of favour, the meaning of words changing and new words entering common usage every year. Just take a look at some old movies to see how significantly language has altered over the past few decades. In the 1930s a female movie star could blithely enquire of a man sitting and talking to her, 'Are you making love to me?' These days she would ask, 'Are you coming on to me?' or something along those lines. And it is highly unlikely that any actress these days would have to ask if she was being made love to or, indeed, would have the spare time to make the enquiry.

Every industry and endeavour has its own jargon and every passing year throws up new buzzwords and jargon. Some common ground needs to be found that will also survive fashion trends. The basic common ground you will need is correct language, with accurate grammar and spelling.

Another thing to keep in mind is that, especially if writing for younger children, your work will form part of that child's education. An enthusiastic person with poor language skills may get far, but probably not so far as they might if their language skills were better. These skills give confidence both to the user and to the person on the receiving end.

At the publishing house the person who receives your work is likely to be someone educated up to, and possibly beyond, university level. Their language knowledge should be good, and their expectations high. A submission littered with spelling mistakes and grammatical inaccuracies will be less highly regarded than a professionally produced piece. A stunningly brilliant idea scribbled on the back of an envelope might prove an exception, but on the whole your approach must be completely *professional*!

Almost every publisher we contacted commented on the spelling and the grammatical content of the scripts and submission (or covering) letters they receive. Here are some of their comments:

Call me pedantic, but it's immediately off-putting to receive a badly presented, misspelt, grammatically incorrect manuscript. Ask someone to check your spelling!

Badly written letters, or proposals containing poor spelling and punctuation usually get rejected. If a writer is incapable of checking an introductory letter then there's precious little chance that he/she is going to take care over a manuscript.

Spelling mistakes. It makes my blood boil when I see really common mistakes like there/their and apostrophes in the wrong places.

Improving your language skills

In Exercise 4, we asked you to produce a piece of writing. What we would like you to do now is to show it to someone whose language skills you trust.

This person may be a friendly teacher whom you know, or someone with an indigenous language degree, or similar expertise. Give them a couple of pages of your work and ask them to go through it, highlighting with absolute honesty any problem areas they find. Explain to them that it is not the *content* that you would like them to examine, but the grammatical accuracy.

If you have no school or college qualifications, are dyslexic or already aware that your writing lacks polish, then there are various ways in which you can get help.

Further education

First there is further education. There are adult education language courses to suit everyone's ability and pocket. These may be run through local schools and colleges. In such classes you will find people of your own level of ability who are willing and enthusiastic to learn. You will also meet teachers who really *want* to teach you. If you have grim memories of your own schooldays, just remember that every student you will encounter is there because they want to be there and because they want to *learn*. Not only will you be polishing your craft, but you will be meeting new people and storing up some new experiences for your Ideas File.

If, for any reason, you are unable to attend classes outside your own home, then there are correspondence and online courses available. These are advertised in newspapers and magazines, and on websites, and range from private companies to recognized correspondence universities with radio, television and summer-school lectures. Private editorial help is also available through writers' magazines, directories of freelance editors and children's writing organizations.

Always try to check the credentials of any person or organization to whom you submit work. Word of mouth is obviously the best recommendation, so ask around to ensure you are getting value for money.

We said earlier that writing can be a lonely business, but you will have noticed by now that the world of writing is teeming with possible contacts and with people from whom advice and encouragement can be obtained.

There are also creative writing organizations and societies that run workshops, lectures and creative writing weeks. Writers' groups and adult education creative writing courses may also be taking place near where you live. These can be wonderfully stimulating and beneficial: you may be set tasks, be asked to read out your work in front of the class, discuss your own and others' work, and have your writing corrected if it needs it.

Should you have been writing in private until now, the thought of presenting your work in public may be very daunting. On the other hand, you may be eager to get up in front of an audience and share your work with them. Either way, you are going to need to develop a thick skin. Your writings are your *babies*, the fruits of your heart and soul, the result of days, weeks and months of effort. No matter how you view your writing, it is certainly going to be very personal to you and revealing it in an open forum will be a major – and for some, traumatic – experience.

How good are you at dealing with criticism?

Throughout your writing career you will *have* to deal with rejections and put-downs. Do think carefully before you choose to present your work in public. Perhaps you need to give yourself a little more time to hone your skills and temper your spirit. Do not run before you can walk, and do not allow a potential talent to be crushed before it has the chance to blossom.

In a creative writing class, it is always a good idea to keep an open mind about criticism and advice. Ask yourself about the publication history of the person advising or criticizing you. If this person has had only the one book published, say, 40 years ago, on techniques in postmodernist beekeeping, then you might wonder whether this person is really in any position to comment on your brilliant new idea for a young adult novel or pre-school picture book.

Believe in yourself, but keep in mind the needs and requirements of the market. If you have an absolute brainwave of an idea, do *not* discuss it with other people: they might very well sneak off and write it themselves whether deliberately or subconsciously. The benefits to be gained from further education or from creative writing classes will be to have your writing skills checked and improved as well as stimulating your creativity, *not* to give away your best ideas.

It is not enough to feel confident of your language; you also need to be able to present your work in an acceptable fashion. Stories circulate occasionally of some idiot *savant* whose barely legible scribbles on the back of breakfast cereal packets are snapped up by a publisher and transformed into a novelty bestseller. As far as *this* book is concerned, such unusual events are irrelevant to the fact that *your* work *must* be presented to a publisher in a professional way.

Can you type?

'Professional' means in the form of black type on white A4 paper, and/or on computer disc. The finer points of professional presentation will be dealt with in Chapter 9, but meanwhile, can you type? If you cannot, then life is going to be difficult, and it will definitely benefit you to learn.

Certainly you could employ a professional freelance typist to produce your final copy, but this approach has distinct disadvantages: it is expensive; it means you will not be able to do any last-minute fine-tuning; and if the manuscript needs to be revised, a fresh copy will be required (yet more expense).

You may have a friend who can type. Three or four manuscripts/revisions down the line, you may not! On the whole, it is far better for you to acquire the skill yourself. Typing and keyboard skills courses are available through adult education classes, schools, correspondence courses, software packages for computers, and from teach-yourself-at-home workbooks. You will be able to learn at your own pace. (If you are presently a two-fingered typist, you could improve your keyboard skills, speed and accuracy and, moreover, prevent the very real risk of repetitive strain injury.) It may mean going back to basics, of course, and unlearning all those bad habits, but the results would be worth the effort.

Tools of the trade

Your work might begin with notes scribbled on slips and scraps of paper. You might have a notebook or a sheaf of lined writing paper, but however you get down to the business of writing out your ideas, you need to make yourself comfortable both in terms of your environment and the tools you use.

Roald Dahl would exile himself to a shed at the bottom of his garden. J. K. Rowling used a series of cafés. J. R. R. Tolkien commented that he could not put a word to paper until he was all but obscured in a fug of pipe smoke.

Pen and paper

If you choose to write first in longhand, then you may have a favourite old pencil, or a fountain pen or black ballpoint pen. Use whatever instrument suits you best.

If you use lined paper, then leave a gap of at least one line between your writing. This will help you when you come to revise your work. It may help to do revisions in a different colour pen, as this will show you how your work has developed. Provide yourself with wide margins and write only on one side of the paper: the reverse will give you additional space for alterations and additions.

Computers

A computer is your most expensive option, but you may feel that the benefits outweigh the cost, especially if you have children or other people in your household who will be able to take advantage of it.

Once again, before you dash out with your credit card/cheque book/ sock full of cash, you need to do some research. For a start, introduction to computer courses are widely available and will help you get some idea of the kind of system most suitable to your needs.

Find yourself a reputable retail outlet with knowledgeable staff and a good after-care service. Word of mouth, once again, is as good a recommendation as any. Finances willing, you should buy the best system you can afford. The idea of being confronted by a CD-ROM or modem may fill you with trepidation, but as anyone who uses computers will tell you, there is nothing like playing with them to get to know them, and when you are comfortable with the technology, a whole world of opportunities will open to you.

Extras such as modems are becoming essential. An editor in urgent need of, say, your biographical details could ask you to e-mail it to them in time for the meeting where the decision as to whether or not your work will be bought is being discussed. It could make all the difference. One day, you could be building your own website to publicize your own work worldwide. It is worth thinking about, and it is well worth your while to find out more, through journals and computer-literate friends. Radio and television programmes are also a good source of up-to-the-minute information.

Save your work!

If you are using a computer, it is vitally important that you remember to save your work as you go along. At the end of each writing session, copy your work onto a separate backup disc which should then be labelled and dated, and/or print it out. Keep your work discs and your printed typescripts in a safe, element-proof place.

Many experienced writers have lost hours of work because they forgot to save their efforts regularly. If the phone rings, save your work before picking up the receiver. If the doorbell rings, save your work before you move to answer it. Basically, save any work before you leave your machine for whatever reason! It does not take long for a cat to leap onto your keyboard and tread on the delete key, thus jettisoning an entire morning's work. Nor does it take more than a second or two for a small, helpful child to switch your machine off. If you set your computer to save your work automatically every 15 minutes, then even a major problem like a power cut need not be a total disaster.

Insurance

You should have accident insurance cover for your computer. Some household contents policies may cover such items, but some do not. Also, some buildings insurance policies do not cover your home if it is also your workplace, especially if you occasionally receive business visitors, or your name is published. Authors, check your cover!

It is also important to have your computer insured in case anything goes wrong with it. Purchase an extended service warranty when you buy your machine. The last thing you need is an inoperative machine and the prospect of a large bill to get it repaired, not to mention the delay and inconvenience of finding someone to repair it. Remember, it is important to get your computer up and running again as quickly as possible – without it you may not be able to work.

Reference books

There are many books available which can help you with your writing. Authors' societies may have recommended reading lists. You may wish to start off with one or two 'beginner's guides' and then expand your collection as your interests and needs evolve.

Three books will be of particular value.

A dictionary

A dictionary is essential. If you can afford only one dictionary to begin with, then you should buy an up-to-date dictionary. Do not borrow your great-uncle's school dictionary: language changes quickly. A simple contemporary dictionary should be sufficient for your writing needs, and some browsing through the pages may well open your eyes to what words are now in common use and are considered an acceptable part of the language.

A thesaurus

A thesaurus can be very useful when you are stuck for the exact word you need, or if you want to avoid repeating a word or phrase. A thesaurus will provide you with lists of alternatives to keep your writing sharp and sparkling with interest. Seek the advice of a bookseller or librarian on which thesaurus will best suit your needs.

A writer's reference book

Any one of the annually updated writer's reference books contain enormous amounts of useful information, from publishers' and literary agents' addresses, to prize awards and guidelines on copyright.

Spell-checkers

Ode to spell checkers
I have a spelling checker
I disk covered four my PC.
It plane lee marks four my revue
Miss steaks aye can knot see.

A checker is a blessing.
It freeze yew lodes of thyme.
It helps me right awl stiles two reed,
And aides me when aye rime.

— Author unknown

A spell-checker on your computer is a great asset. However, these are not always sufficient or workable. For instance, a spell-checker cannot differentiate between words such as 'bear' and 'bare' which could be potentially embarrassing, not to mention 'there' and 'their'.

It is also as well to check whether your system has an American English spelling list. Many words are spelt differently in Britain and America. You can set the spell-checker dictionary to the appropriate language.

Also, if you are checking a long piece of work which contains made-up words or names, or a non-fiction text full of abbreviations or unusual words, then a spell-checker will have a field-day highlighting the whole lot and you will be left to laboriously explain to your machine that all these words are okay, and to add them to the dictionary software.

Never rely totally on your spell-checker for accuracy. Read through your work yourself, too.

Raising funds

One young author on a very limited budget asked her friends and family to help her by supplying her with writing materials in lieu of birthday and Christmas presents. This is not only very helpful, but such a show of support will lift the morale of an ambitious budding author.

If you are unable to afford a computer, then perhaps you can borrow one or have access to one through work, college or a friend when the time comes to type up a completed work.

Keep all your receipts for anything you spend money on in direct connection with your writing work. This not only includes paper, ink and so on, but also travelling expenses if, say, you visit a museum for research purposes, or for any books you may purchase to help you with a writing project. (See the section, 'Tax and accounts', in Chapter 12.)

Bursaries

Bursaries may be available from arts councils or charitable trusts to enable authors to complete a specific project. Conditions vary: money may be made available to a new author, or to an established author who wishes to concentrate on a particular project which would be considered to be of great potential value to the reading public. A fairly detailed explanation of the planned project would be needed, along with some supporting references from people whose opinion would be taken seriously by the judges in the relevant decision-making panel. Such grants and bursaries can be quite large sums of money, enough to enable an author to give up a day job for several months in order to complete a project.

Details are available through libraries, authors' magazines, in writers' reference books and on many websites.

Creating the space and the time

You have set up your Ideas File. You have done lots of research. You have learnt to type, and you have access to a computer, pen and paper, or whatever. So, what do you need next before you can start work?

Two things:

- ■ Space in which to write
- ■ Time in which to write.

The ideal situation would be to have your own writing space, an area used for nothing else. Some authors have a spare room they can use. Others convert lofts or sheds into an organized (or disorganized) office: computer on desk, comfortable writing table, typist's chair and bookshelf with dictionary, thesaurus and other books at arm's reach. (To many authors, this scenario would be paradise on earth!)

Whatever space you can squeeze out of the general maelstrom of your living space, try to make it as comfortable and convenient for yourself as possible. You cannot be creative if you are too hot, too cold, too cramped or crammed into an uncomfortable chair or trying to write on a washing machine in spin mode.

Some authors conduct their business from bed; others work at the kitchen table or a desk in a hallway or under the stairs. Wherever you work, aim to make it somewhere as peaceful as possible so that you are able to concentrate (even if your idea of peace includes Wagner operas as background music).

One full-time author got so stir-crazy from being constantly on his own at home that he ended up hiring a desk in the corner of a busy office just so he felt that he was keeping in touch with the real world (which proves that peace is a pretty flexible concept). Other authors need absolute silence and solitude if they are going to be able to function at all. The least interruption can close the brain down for hours.

The telephone can certainly drive authors crazy. Imagine: you are in the middle of a complex piece of writing when the telephone rings. You pick it up, have a conversation that lasts only a couple of minutes, and then return to your desk only to find you cannot remember for the life of you what was going to happen next.

Make it clear to friends and relations that working at home does not mean you can be called up every half-hour for a quick chat. A five-minute telephone call can result in the creative part of your brain being scrambled for an hour or more. If you have a real problem with this, then you might be wise to disconnect the telephone for the duration of your writing stint. Alternatively, put the telephone out of earshot, bury it in the garden or, if you can, buy an answerphone or messaging service and let it take messages until you have finished work.

If you are able to allocate a regular daily or weekly time for writing, then make sure *everyone* is in no doubt that at those times you are to be left alone, short of winning the lottery or the house catching fire. Ask friends not to drop by for a chat. Tell your partner or your children that you require to be *invisible* for *x* amount of time. If all else fails, insert earplugs and lock yourself in your room!

> *At times when the need to write is strong, there's no problem.*
> *If there are problems with characters or you're feeling your*
> *way with the plot, it's harder and more intermittent. I try to*
> *write something every day, even if it's only a few words, just*
> *to keep in touch with the story.*

Create a space where you can leave your work and know it will be unmolested. It could be somewhere as simple as a drawer or an out-of-pets-and-children's-reach shelf. Wherever it is, keep it as organized as you can: it does you no favours if it takes you half an hour to get yourself organized every time you want to return to your work. Get into the habit of putting everything away in an organized and accessible fashion every time you stop working.

You do not want to lose the scrap of paper on which you jotted the brilliant but complicated best-selling idea that came to you in the middle of the night. Keep it somewhere safe. Similarly, you do not want your finished manuscript to arrive on a publisher's desk covered in coffee stains, muddy paw-prints or smears of marmalade from a midday snack. An organized approach should prevent all the above problems.

> *The nearer to the deadline, the more disciplined I become. Inspiration usually comes to me whilst I am writing, and often I have to force myself. I don't have set times for writing because of other commitments.*

You should treat writing in the same way as you would treat studying for an examination. Create a writing routine. If you try to fit it in now and then, you will probably find the 'thens' out-number the 'nows'. Pick a time when your mind is at its most alert. If your brain is a seething cauldron of creativity first thing in the morning, try to set aside an hour before you go to work, or before the rest of your household awakes.

Perhaps your mind sparks best when you return from work: try to devote an hour or so to writing before you do anything else. Perhaps your inventiveness peaks late at night – a time when you are less likely to be derailed by telephone calls or ringing doorbells. Perhaps weekend mornings provide you with the peace you need.

Your individual circumstances will dictate when you can write; the important thing is to fight for your writing time and to make it an absolute habit, breakable by friends and family only on pain of swift retribution.

Some authors make it a point to produce one finished page per day. That may not sound like much, but do that for one year and you are looking at a 365-page book! Other full-time authors set themselves specific deadlines, this being the only way they can push themselves to complete a piece of work.

> *I have to be pushed by a deadline to write at all. It's not a regular thing, and I seldom write anything out of the blue. Publisher's requirements are always foremost in my mind.*

> *I sit down at 8.30 every day and stay seated until 5.30 every day – except for lunch break, tea breaks, coffee breaks, loo breaks, nip down to the shops and get something absolutely essential like a tube of fruit gums breaks ...*

Getting ideas

Authors get their ideas from absolutely everywhere, but it may help if we divide the harvesting areas into three main categories.

First-hand

First-hand ideas include things experienced by you personally, or things which happen to people very close to you. They can be events from your own childhood, or from any time in your life, where the experience would relate to something which you could use as the starting point for a project – for instance, sibling rivalry between you and a sister/brother, or between you and close friends. These experiences will range from the traumatic to the hilarious, but the important thing for you to do is to swim back though your life and try to revive your feelings of the time.

- Why was it an absolute scream when your teacher sat on that boiled egg you slipped onto her chair?
- How did you feel when your best friend went to live in another part of the country?
- What was the impact on your life when your parents separated?

Use your own life as an Ideas File. Delve back and into yourself: your experiences may one day help another child to understand his/her own situation, and to realize that other people have had the same problems.

Perhaps you notice that your own child is afraid of thunderstorms. What might help? A picture book, possibly, which explains exactly what thunder and lightning is and why there is no reason to be scared.

If you are a parent, or have regular contact with children, the important thing is to see things from a child's perspective. Adults frequently believe that *their* wishes and opinions should take precedence over those of a child. If you are going to write for children, you must forget all about that. The priorities of children are quite different from those of an adult. Not less important, just *different*.

For example, children perceive time in a very different way from adults. Half an hour can seem like an eternity to a child. The agonizing, anticipatory wait of two whole weeks for a birthday party to take place can reduce a child to a tearful, gibbering wreck on the actual day. You must try to remember what this felt like if you are going to speak believably to children through your work.

Books for young adults often explore the gulf in understanding between parents and children. You can tackle this only if you enter the world of the young person and address the conflict from his/her point of view. Try to remember the battles you had as a teenager with those adults who wielded authority over you, be they parents, teachers, the police or whomever. How did *you* feel when these people tried to impose their will on you?

Remember your own feelings of enchantment when you were a small child. Think back to the time when quite small things held an entire world of fascination. A walk in a wood where *anything* could be lurking. A secret tunnel known only to you and your friends. The first time you noticed the shadows on the moon. Faces in flames and the shapes to be found in clouds. Desperate alliances and sundered friendships.

The lives of children teem with imperatives. Who is your best friend? Who do you hate in the world? Children live on the brink of triumph and disaster minute by minute. You need to live it with them. Never be squeamish: dive in!

Second-hand

Second-hand experiences are those that are repeated to you or observed by you, but which do not directly involve you. Such experiences could include, say, an overheard conversation between children on a bus or a train, or happenings related to you by friends or relations.

Obviously you are going to be one step removed from the intensity of such experiences, but your job as an author is to soak up all the elements, be they comic or tragic, and to tuck them into your Ideas File for future reference.

It may be that a single aspect of someone's anecdote sets your story antennae twitching, a throwaway comment that is hardly relevant to the main thrust of the story but which strikes you as having potential. A word of warning here: not everyone relishes the idea that everything they say to you is just grist for your writing mill. If you hear a story which you just *know* is a sure-fire winner, then make some judicious changes. Adapt it, maybe by changing the sex of the main protagonists, altering the location, making changes in their social background. Create new characters from aspects of several different people. Edit the story so that the heart of it – the spark the ignited your interest – is still there, but construct around that, a world created in your own imagination. (We will mention libel in Chapter 9.)

Perhaps you notice some piece of social behaviour between children which you find interesting, intriguing or amusing. Jot it down and file it away.

Be particularly aware of the rhythm and dynamics of speech. A good rule of thumb for an author is to keep the mouth shut and the ears open. Listen to the way people speak.

Take an 8-year-old child: how does he/she speak to friends? How does he/she speak to children he/she does not know? How does he/she speak to older children? To younger children? How does he/she speak to adults – parents/guardians/authority figures? It will not take long for you to notice that children use a multitude of differing modes of speech, adapting themselves to their circumstances in a very sophisticated way. A sweet-faced little cherub may be very polite and biddable in front of adults, but may mutate into a bullying, screaming banshee once let loose among his or her peers.

A few words of advice concerning dialogue. The only way you are going to be able to write convincing dialogue is by listening to real people talking to one another. Do not try to learn this from books, television shows, films or radio. In all these media, a filtration and editing process has already taken place. You need conversation in the raw, untouched by any other writer's hand. When you have written a piece of speech, read it aloud to check if it feels right in your mouth and whether it sounds natural when it hits the air.

Third-hand

The third-hand areas from which you can get ideas are those where you have no personal contact with the story at all. They split into two sub-headings.

Reported

You may notice an item on a television news programme which takes your interest. You may read the report of an incident in a newspaper, or hear of a real event via the radio.

> *A missing 8-year-old boy was rescued today from the basement of a part-demolished building following a two-day search. He was exhausted but unharmed, having fallen through rotting floorboards whilst exploring with a friend. The delay in discovering the boy was due to the fact that his friend was too scared to tell his parents of the incident as they had been specifically told to keep away from the demolition site.*

This story is adapted from a real incident reported in a television programme. From an author's point of view, it has several areas of interest. There is the incident itself, of course, written as a kind of adventure, but an author will be interested in what was going through the minds of the two boys at the time. One trapped in the dark, the other just as trapped by the fear of recriminations. And then you have that moment when the second boy finally had to tell his parents what had happened. Powerful stuff!

How about taking the lives of the two boys on a few years, and writing a story of them as teenagers? What sort of effect would that incident have on their future relationship? How will the second boy be coping with his feelings of guilt that his delay in telling the truth could easily have been the cause of the other boy's death? What if these two boys are interested in the same girl? Might the boy who was trapped use the story to put the girl off the other boy?

As you can see, the possibilities are endless, and all this from a fleeting snippet of news, jotted down and filed away when everyone else had forgotten all about it by the next day.

Similarly, headlines, odd paragraphs and photographs clipped from newspapers and magazines can prove to have enormous potential.

There is a phenomenon called 'cab-driver's eye' which is used to explain the way in which a cruising taxi driver's eyes are constantly swivelling around in search of a potential fare. You should learn to cultivate 'author's eye'.

Refried

Whereas the previous section on reported events concerned itself with real incidents reported through the media, the *refried* third-hand area is where you glean ideas from other authors.

We need to be perfectly clear what we are talking about here. Stealing other people's ideas is not only cheating, it is also illegal. It is called plagiarism and must be avoided. However, this does not mean your own imagination cannot be sparked by something that happens in a book, play, movie, television or radio programme you happen across.

For example, one author wrote a book which told the story of 'mad' Mrs Rochester from *Jane Eyre*. Mrs Rochester was a shadowy figure kept incarcerated in the attic of the house whose main contribution to the story comes when she escapes and burns the house down. Having read *Jane Eyre*, this author found herself wondering what it must have been like to have been that locked-away woman, and thus her book was born. Likewise, a playwright took a single, almost throwaway comment in a Shakespeare play and wrote a play of his own based upon it.

Consider myths, legends and fairy tales. These tales have survived because they tell a riveting story which has the ability to transcend changes in society, sometimes over many centuries. If you are short of ideas, you could do a lot worse than read a book of Greek, Japanese, Aztec or Russian folk tales and legends.

'Sleeping Beauty' could be brought up to date and written as a story of a girl in a coma and how her boyfriend copes with the situation. 'The Ugly Duckling' is the universally understood story of any child who learns to throw off some burden and be themselves. One editor to whom we spoke commented that Verdi's opera *Rigoletto* had provided at least two storylines for a well-known American teen-fiction book series.

By now you will have realized that every single thing that you see or hear can have potential for your work, be it in the world of fiction, non-fiction or education. All you need to do is reach out and grab it, file it and personalize it.

Gathering information and storing it

Have you considered investing in one of those pocket-cassette recorders? You may find it more convenient to simply *speak* an idea into the machine rather than write it down. Otherwise, a small notebook or diary will do the job as an initial holding-pen for your daily observations, thoughts and ideas. A personal organizer (paper or electronic) can also be used, although you may find it a little bulky for everyday use, whereas a slimline notebook will slip conveniently into a pocket or bag. Whatever method you use for recording your fieldwork, you will ultimately want to bring your findings home and make use of them in your Ideas File.

Dr Johnson said that there are two kinds of knowledge: the knowledge which a person carries around in his/her head; and the equally important knowledge of where to *find things out*. One of the points of your Ideas File is to save you the trouble and potential heartache of trying to carry everything around in your head but, more importantly, the material you have accumulated must be easily accessible.

Be professional in your approach to storing your Ideas File. We mentioned earlier the possibilities of a drawer or large envelope. This is all very well if your research is minimal and based on a single project, but if you are (and you *should* be) engaging in a permanent general trawl for ideas, then you will very rapidly find yourself with a towering heap of paper which takes an age to delve through.

The perfect solution to this problem is, of course, a proper filing cabinet with a sophisticated index system. This may not be as far out of your reach as you might think, providing you have the space. Ex-office filing cabinets, from small, two-drawer affairs to five- or six-drawer giants, can often be purchased relatively cheaply in second-hand office-supply stores. Or again, you could take a look at one of the many 'selling' magazines. An office clearance could land you a real bargain.

Failing this, a drawer in a desk would do the job, or even a drawer in an ordinary cabinet or chest of drawers, provided everyone is told that the said drawer is not to be stuffed with socks, pieces of motorbike engine or any other old junk. There are also box-filing systems available in stationery stores, in which a fair amount of information can be kept tidily.

The important thing is to implement a system which you understand, be it alphabetical, numerical or cross-referenced, on paper or computer. You could have files for specific projects and files of general interest items. A separate file for pictures and another for newspaper cuttings. Files of character ideas and files of storyline jottings.

If your project is a non-fiction or educational one, you may wish to subdivide your work into topic or chapter headings, and store information that way.

Remember, careful planning at this stage will save you a lot of trouble in the long run. If you planned on decorating a room, you would need to get everything in order before you started – unless you found it entertaining to take a trip down to the local DIY store mid-work with a length of pasted paper in your in arms and a perplexed expression on your face. Writing is exactly the same. Some well-considered preparatory work will help you enormously when you come to actually sit down and get the project started.

Exercise 5

After all that concentrated information, a pause for some light relief. One author told us that to get ideas, he often turns common situations on their heads, or headlines from newspapers or television back to front. For example, a newspaper headline, 'Lottery hoaxer fools family' becomes 'Family fools lottery hoaxer', and a storyline is born! Write out some ideas (fiction or non-fiction) or cut out headlines, cut them up into word-sized chunks and juggle them around. This is an excellent activity if you have a creative block. If an idea emerges, sketch it out now, before you read on!

4 | DECIDING WHAT TO WRITE

You may already have very definite thoughts about the areas in which you want to write. You may have an imagination overflowing with ideas about tap-dancing octopi, flying furniture or ghostly gladioli with which you hope to capture and enrapture your young audience and thus make a fortune. Your intended work may be a brilliant new way of explaining the human respiratory system in words and pictures or enlightening your potential audience about glass-blowing as a leisure activity. In whatever direction your aspirations are leading you, there must have been some initial spark which made you sit bolt upright in bed one night or suddenly go glassy-eyed in the middle of a conversation and realize you wanted to write.

You may not yet be aware of the astonishing diversity of the children's market. There is an obvious division into *fiction* and *non-fiction*, but that is like dividing all animal life into land-dwellers and water-dwellers. The truth is much more complex.

Fiction

How is fiction defined? One renowned author was asked by some intellectuals to define 'the novel'. They were probably hoping for some obscure observations which they could take away with them to ponder at length. However, the author thought for a moment and then came back with the comment, 'It's telling a story'. The delightful thing about this response is that it pricks pomposity as well as hitting the spot.

The point of fiction is to tell a story, any story, in a way that will hold the attention of the audience. Story-telling is as old as humanity itself. No matter how far back you research into human history, you will always discover the relics of story-telling, from the aboriginal cave paintings in Australia to the hieroglyphs on the walls of Egyptian tombs.

In many cultures the tale-bearer was an important person. In ancient Rome, poets would be hired to tell elevating tales of the behaviour and misbehaviours of gods and goddesses, as well as recounting, in verse, the deeds of more earthly heroes. In those days, oratory was a great skill, especially in cultures where the average person did not read or write, and the maintenance of a cohesive social structure was reliant on people who could tell stories which bound people together by way of a common story-telling ancestry.

The earliest stories, as far as we know, were usually attempts at explaining events and phenomena beyond ordinary understanding. You could almost think of them as *science fiction*: they were attempts at making sense of the world in a way with which the human brain could cope. How do the seasons of the world change, and why? What forces are at work changing the shape of the moon? What is lightning? Who tows the sun across the sky and where does it go at night? If you sail beyond the horizon, what will happen to you? What wonders or terrors lie beyond the sealed doors of death?

On the white, outer edges of old maps were written the words 'Here be dragons', but someone somewhere first to had invent the idea of dragons, just as someone somewhere created the idea of flying horses, magic rings and gorgons with serpents for hair. Equally, someone else invented androids and 'warp drive' and little green people from Mars who disembark from flying saucers and ask petrol pumps to take them to their leaders. And you never know, you *might* invent something that will fascinate readers 500 years hence. After all, *someone* has to come up with this generation's marvels. There is one thing in this world that flies beyond all boundaries, and that thing is the human imagination.

Without getting too philosophical, the idea of the difference between 'fact' and 'truth' can be explored within the bounds of fiction. A myth or legend concerning the activities of Greek gods may not be factual, but it contains an enormous amount of *truth*. It is apparent in many religions that the gods and goddesses frequently behave in ways that are all too human. They are capable of being devious, brutal, aggressive, compassionate, arrogant, loving, angry, stupid, thoughtful, selfish, brave and cowardly.

Myths, legends, parables and fables all have a similar root: they seek to enlighten whilst entertaining. And the more an audience is *entertained* the more likely that audience is to remember the kernel of truth at the heart of a rip-roaring yarn. This balance between enlightenment and entertainment leads us neatly on to a very salient point in writing for children: the best way to convey a message is to give the impression that no message is being conveyed.

You may be deeply concerned about the environment, or wish to warn young people about the dangers of drug abuse; you may think a little morality needs to be introduced into children's behaviour. Children can spot didacticism and moralizing from miles away! You would be amazed at how speedily a child can vanish if someone is telling them something that is perceived as 'being good for them'.

A story can be of value, even if it contains no social message or moral at all. It can be valuable as pure escapism. It can simply be *fun*. Children's writing certainly forms an aspect of their education, but that does not mean children should not read simply for pleasure. After all, even if the story is just a piece of escapist lunacy, the child will still be absorbing aspects of grammar, punctuation and syntax.

> *I get my ideas from books, television, characters and situations in myths and legends, and from using archetypal storylines.*
>
> *Useful plot starters are folk and fairy tales, legends and stories of old.*

The good thing about myths, legends and fairy tales is that their universality gives them the power to be constantly reinvented to suit each new generation. Ghost stories have lost none of their power despite the strides of science and physics to prove (or disprove) their existence. In days past, ghosts haunted the wild woods or distant, crumbling towers; these days, they lurk in office buildings and drive spectral cars down streets in the twilight.

In brief, the business of fiction is to present an audience with something that is 'truthful' (that is, believable or at least capable of creating a willing suspension of disbelief), but not based on *fact*. The Greeks had Ulysses; the Norsemen had Beowulf; the Anglo-Saxons had Robin Hood – all maverick, mythical heroes. The twenty-first century has Charlie's Angels, Gladiator, Buffy the Vampire Slayer, X-Men and, still, James Bond.

Categories of fiction

Fiction breaks down into several categories. Publishers are always on the look out for modern-day humour. If you can write page-turning contemporary stories that make people laugh, your chances of being published are healthy.

Then there is fantasy, sword-and-sorcery, horror, scary/ghost stories and science fiction. The common thread in these areas is that they take the audience outside the accepted laws of nature, to an elven city, a wizard's chamber, a werewolf's lair or a desert planet beyond Betelgeuse. As the market is already saturated with such books, you will need to come up with something startlingly original if you want get published in this category.

Historical fiction is another category of fiction (but think twice before embarking on yet another telling of the legend of King Arthur). A story of children caught up, say, in the French Revolution will need to be heavily researched and very accurate. Even then, the most meticulously researched and presented story may not find a publisher in such a limited area. If the area of history you have chosen is being studied by children at school, your chances of interesting a publisher increase. However, in historical fiction the story must come first. The text should not read like a documentary with the addition of token fictional characters.

Romantic fiction can draw a large young adult audience, as can thrillers and crime stories. Research your market, looking at different publishers and their series to get a sense of the range of acceptable styles and limitations. Romance can range from growing friendship to potential parenthood, from historical to contemporary settings.

Publishers are always on the look out for 'series' ideas (that is, an idea in which a regular cast of characters will appear in a succession of books). Enid Blyton's *Famous Five* books are an example of this sort of thing, and have been given a new lease of life in spin-off series such as *The Adventures of George*. More recently, series such as *Buffy*, *Dawson's Creek*, *Vampire Vigilanties*, *Donkey Diaries*, *Animal Ark* and many more sell a lot of books by allowing an audience to follow the ongoing exploits of well-known or established characters.

Series books follow the adage of 'giving the public what they want', by variations on particular themes. Such books can safely be bought in the knowledge that they will involve known characters in known situations.

There is also call for poetry and plays for use in schools, as well as themed poetry collections for the general trade market. Poetry has never been an easy area for new authors to make their mark. You may need to establish yourself on the poetry scene first (via competitions, readings, poetry circles, etc.).

In the young adult market you will find a certain amount of *issue-fiction*, in which contemporary social issues are explored. Such books have to be of a very high standard if they are to find a home in the limited market area.

Non-fiction

The range for non-fiction work is enormous: it can cover anything from a short piece in a magazine to a multi-volume encyclopedia.

You may have noticed that your own children are interested in watching tadpoles transform into frogs. You decide to write a piece explaining both the various stages of the transformation and outlining the optimum ways of looking after them. Add some information on amphibians in general, a few thoughts on their dietary habits and the environment in which they best flourish; mix in a series of diagrams, illustrations and photographs, and you are well on the way to developing one of those 'How to Look After Your First ...' books that are found in bookshops, supermarkets, libraries and pet stores everywhere.

Alternatively, you may be an expert juggler. How better to pass on your skill and knowledge to children than by writing everything down in an article or a short book? Juggling could be put into a wider context – the performing arts, for instance. Your piece on juggling could become but a single chapter in a book about street theatre or the circus. A skilful juggling mathematician could even incorporate juggling into an explanation of the laws of probability and calculus. A biologist could use juggling to introduce a work on how it is that the human body is capable of such dexterity.

Any and every activity under the sun is capable of generating its own non-fiction guide. How to play football. How to use face-paints. How to make cookies. How to find bugs and where to keep them. How telephones work and how to use one. How to build a magic castle out of empty toilet rolls and discarded egg-boxes. How to cope with the measles and why you became ill in the first place.

History

Who built the great pyramids of Egypt? Who invented gunpowder? What sparked the American Civil War? When did men first travel to the moon and back?

Geography

Where is Egypt and why did its ancient peoples rely so heavily on the annual flooding of the Nile? What is the Great Wall of China and why was it built? What happens when an agricultural society meets with an industrial one?

Science

How were the pyramids built by a society that had not even invented the wheel? What are the component parts of cement and how does it hold buildings together? How did people manage to get a rocket to the moon?

As you can see, non-fiction subjects can be viewed in a multiplicity of ways, and each viewpoint is a potential piece of work for the enquiring author (be that person a teacher, an interested parent, an expert, or just someone who wants to find something out for themselves and then share their knowledge with others).

It is a famous observation that most creative writing starts off with the phrase, 'What if ...' What if there was a book for children explaining DNA (deoxyribonucleic acid – the building blocks of life) in an entertaining, amusing and informative way? Is there?

Areas of non-fiction

It is admittedly early days in this book for a lot of technical information about publishing practices, but it is worth pointing out that non-fiction divides into two main areas: trade non-fiction and educational non-fiction. An author would need to investigate both markets before embarking on any project, as they both have quite different and separate requirements.

Trade non-fiction includes those books or articles in magazines (or indeed specialist magazines) which you might buy for home consumption. Trade non-fiction includes everything, in fact, from the 'Life → This Way' teenage self-help kind of book to the hugely successful, fun non-fiction titles of the 'Triffic Chocolate' and 'Horrible History' variety. Trade non-fiction will appeal to the general market, as well as school purchasers.

Educational non-fiction is primarily bought by schools and colleges for educational purposes. These can range from reading schemes to foreign language workbooks. These books will have been commissioned with the school curriculum needs specifically in mind.

Faction

As this hybrid word suggests, 'faction' is the skilful combination of fiction and non-fiction. Most people will have encountered this method of story-telling via films or television mini-series which dramatize the life and loves of Marilyn Monroe, or the lives, loves, divorces and beheadings of Henry VIII's six wives. Anything which purports to shed light on a historical character or event in a dramatized form is actually 'faction', be it the life of Gandhi, the Battle of the Bulge or the events surrounding the Apollo 13 space mission.

Books in the faction area include historical 'I was there'-type works in which the author 'sees' great events through contemporary eyes. This can be a very effective way of bringing historical subjects vividly to life, although, as with all non-fiction areas, thorough research is vital. An Egyptian child, riding on a bicycle to watch the building of the Great Pyramid of Cheops might raise eyebrows even in the realms of faction.

Dramatized biographies can also bring past lives into sharp focus, as can dramatized versions of disasters or extraordinary events: the Great Flood, the Irish Potato Famine or the first person to invent the jet engine can all be made more real to young people by giving them a contemporary, dramatized voice. Similarly, a book for very young children about going into hospital, starting school, ballet lessons or learning to swim, can benefit from the faction approach.

Just when you thought the range for children's writing had become bewildering enough, we now throw a few more thoughts at you. What about comic strips? What about children's magazines? How about sticker and activity books, puzzles, painting and colouring? What about original material for first publication on the internet? You should by now have realized exactly how diverse the world of children's writing actually is, and where your book, *Your One Hundred and One Favourite Bathtime Burbles*, will find its warmest welcome.

Language levels and reading ages

You are 7 years old and are spotted by your peers reading a book clearly labelled 'For readers aged 5 and 6'. Your friends are hugely amused by this. What do you do? In all likelihood, you will stop reading this book and in future conspicuously avoid any book that might look as if it is too young for you (whether you like the look of it or not). Possibly you do not need the ridicule of your peers to decide you want nothing to do with books specifically shown as being aimed beneath your age range or, more to the point, below your 'literacy' range. Maybe you do not even want to read books that are aimed at your age group!

At the time when this book was being written, many publishers were still in the habit of dividing their children's lists into very specific reading and interest ages, particularly those aimed at the younger readers. They do this in a variety of ways, from the deliberate inclusion of a target age on the cover to colour-coding or age-coding labels on the jackets, all intended to push their product into the correct pair of hands. Whether this type of categorization is a good idea or not is debatable, but while such methods are being employed, it is important for an author to understand what is going on.

The main reading age groups are divided into the under 5-year-olds, 5–7, 8–12 and 12+. (Publishers often define these groups even more tightly: 2–5, 3–6, 4–7, 5–8, 6–9, 7–10, 8–11, 9–12, 12+.) Some publishers take a more broadly defined colour-coding or series jacket design approach which liberates children from an age-based reading straitjacket. What self-respecting 7-year-old wants to be seen reading a book clearly labelled as being for 6-year-olds? And who exactly makes these reading age distinctions? How relevant are they to real life? Some children are encouraged with words whilst still in the crib, rapidly picking up language from ABC friezes around the bedroom walls, from alphabet cards flashed at them by parents and from nursery education provided both by parents and teachers in the pre-school sector.

Children throughout the world learn to read at different times, at enormously varying speeds and in very different ways. Remember that a book written and published in England could easily end up being read in Russia, Belgium, Korea or Zimbabwe. The majority of children start full-time schooling around the age of 5 and will usually be reading alone and silently by the age of 7. But children's education and reading abilities vary enormously for many reasons, and text which one 7-year-old will discard as too simple may well cause problems for a child of a similar age but of a different reading level. The task of the author is therefore to aim their work squarely at the middle of the appropriate age group and to pick up the average child.

The requirements of publishers for the language and level of books vary so widely that an author must research (yes, that word again) the market and aim his/her work accordingly. For instance, picture books for the very young may consist only of 12 words. Further up the reading scale, an illustrated story book may consist of 2,500 words, and a book aimed at the young adult market could be 50,000 words. There are exceptions to this rule, but it is unwise to present a potential publisher with a book aimed at 12-year-olds which weighs in at 250,000 words.

Another useful tip is that children like to read of the exploits of people slightly older than themselves. So, whatever age range you are seeking to write for, position the leading characters either at the top end of that group, or slightly above it. For readers aged 8–12, the age of the protagonists in your work should be 12+, and a book aimed at 7–10 year-olds should have characters aged mainly between 9 and 11. This is simple psychology and no more demanding than choosing a birthday present that is just a little older than the child for whom it is intended. (Also bear in mind that young adult magazines aimed at the mid- to late teens are actually read by children as young as 10.)

Fluent readers are going to devour everything from picture books, sometimes with a very adult subtext, to books that would generally be thought beyond their ability or interest. C. S. Lewis, the author of many much-loved children's books, observed that his childhood was spent in a house festooned with books of every type, form and nature, some intended for children, and some emphatically not, but that he was denied access to nothing. Given half a chance, an inquisitive 8-year-old could have a field day with a copy of *War and Peace* in much the same way that an 80-year-old might still enjoy the exploits of Pooh Bear and Piglet.

Exercise 6

The average child's ability to comprehend written information changes as that child gets older. As a writer for children, you must be aware of those changes and judge correctly how to approach children of varying ages. To this end, as a useful test of your ability, write a series of letters, all on the same subject and each aimed at a different age group. The subject can be of your own choosing, but make it something that would be of interest to children of all ages – a description of a forthcoming event, pageant, party or holiday.

First write your letter in such a way that it can be read to a pre-school child by a parent or some other adult.

Next, write the same letter for an 8-year-old.

Now write it for a 13-year-old.

Finally, try writing it for a 17-year-old pen-pal from another country whose first language is not your own.

Points to note

Try not to 'talk down' to your audience. A 13-year-old is unlikely to see the funny side of being written to as if they were only 8, and a 17-year-old, despite any limits on grammatical comprehension, will expect to be treated as an adult, so ecstatic descriptions of jellies and finger-painting will not necessarily be appreciated. Similarly, something which may be of great fun to an 8-year-old (a disco-tent at a fête, for example) is unlikely to have much resonance with a 4-year-old.

Your use of language should alter, from being simple and lucid for the youngest audience to more advanced and complex for the older readers. Correspondingly, your terms of reference must shift in perspective to suit the reader's interest level.

If possible, you should get a parent, teacher or indeed a child of the appropriate age to 'criticize' your letters. The latter, of course, is the best way of discovering whether you have hit the mark, but in any event, seek out someone whose opinion has some authority behind it, and then take heed of what you are told. You then could attempt the exercise again in light of what you have learned.

Language styles

He often changed his residence: and during his various travels, while he visited the most celebrated parts of the south of Europe, his admirers in England were indulged with the productions of his powerful and versatile muse: sometimes proudly soaring into the pure regions of taste, breathing noble sentiments and chivalric feelings: at other times, descending into impure voluptuousness, or grovelling in sheer vulgarity.

This extract is a quote about Lord Byron taken from a book of biographies published in 1845. What clues are there to place that huge sentence in its native time? The length of it, for a start. The writer is producing work for an educated readership for whom the style of the description is as important as the information being conveyed. There is also a very particular moral tone being struck.

We spoke to one author who described being accosted by the chairman of a school's board of governors (and would-be author) and told very effusively how much this interlocutor liked semicolons, and how he lamented that modern publishers tended to erase them and break an elegant single, multi-clause sentence into several smaller parts. Semicolons were to this school governor as glacé cherries are to the gourmet; it probably never occurred to him that these 'despised modern publishers' were concerned more with making his writings more understandable than they were with the elegant preservation of his prose.

Two thoughts:

- Always keep your audience in plain sight.
- Brevity is the soul of wit.

Your job is to communicate, *not* to construct soaring conceits of grammatical whimsy. Say what you want to say as lucidly and briefly as you can. (This does not mean blandly, of course.) Telling an engaging story in 800 words is a lot harder than stretching out the same story over 30,000 words.

Exercise 7

You might like to explore the above point by describing the area immediately surrounding you in a sentence of not more than ten words. Take your sentence to another person and see if they can get any real feel for the place that you have described.

This is not as easy as it sounds, and you may wish to try a number of different approaches as you attempt to grasp the essence of the area being described.

Back to Lord Byron: the sentence we quoted was very much of its time. How might a modern, thumbnail biography approach the same subject?

> *He travelled widely in southern Europe, house-hopping continuously and pausing only to send back his latest works to his English admirers. These works ranged from the lofty and noble to the decidedly earthy.*

The above modernization retains all the information of the original and manages it without a single colon or semicolon – whilst halving the length of the original.

A children's author must keep abreast of how language changes. You need to speak directly to a modern audience without falling into several traps. These traps take on two main forms. First, there is the use of contemporary 'slang'. You should be very cautious in your use of idioms. Buzzwords can very quickly fall out of favour, and having a character say 'See you later, alligator' may have sounded very hip in 1962, but today it just sounds silly. For some time children have been using the word 'wicked' to mean 'brilliant', and 'sad' to mean 'stupid', but how long will these idioms last? Think about your language before you people your books with youngsters who use contemporary slang in their dialogue. Your work still needs to make sense in five years' time.

The other trap is to presume that the moral climate in which you are writing is the only acceptable position from which to view events. The biographer of Lord Byron did just that, and take another look at how pompous they sound to today's reader.

You do not have to delve far back into the nineteenth century to see how social opinion has changed. Look at the children's books written in the two or three decades after the Second World War and note the behaviour of the girls and boys portrayed in those classic stories. Television series, too, were equally 'guilty' of stereotyping male and female roles. Women and girls cooked and cleaned, whilst men and boys fought enemies and aliens!

Times have changed, but when did you last read an adventure story in which the hero was in a wheelchair? Or a story where one of the main characters was deaf, not deaf because the deafness was integral to the plot, but simply deaf in the way that people are in real life?

Like the brush-stroke technique of an artist, many authors can be identified by their style, and often the more famous they are, the more obvious will be their stylistic quirks. As an author wishing to be published, you must be wary of 'copying' these individualistic traits. One author to whom we spoke mentioned that he refused to have anything by Alan Bennett in the house for fear that Bennett's style would prove too insidious in his mind and end up colouring his own work.

It is not that you should not learn from other authors, but the trick is to read so widely that you avoid stylistic plagiarism (albeit subconsciously) and seek through the myriad voices that surround you to find a separate and complete voice of your own.

Synopses and chapter outlines

There are as many different ways of approaching synopses as there are authors. You may start off writing completely inspired, winding your characters up and seeing where they take you. Or you may start a story with a vision of a small shark rising from some bathwater and politely but sheepishly asking its way to the Indian Ocean, without much of an idea about what is going to happen next. That is fine to begin with but, if you want to become a professional, you are not going to have the time to write 'wait-and-see' books in which publishers may show no interest once they are finished. You will be wanting to optimize your time, and part of that involves presenting publishers with synopses or at least storylines before you go to the effort of writing the entire book.

Many full-time authors are invited ('commissioned') to produce particular works; that is, they are paid a sum of money (an 'advance') on signature of a contract in which they agree to write a specific book (or a number of books) on a particular topic for a particular readership and of a particular length. Obviously a publisher will want to know what they are getting; hence the author will be asked first to submit a proposal and then more detailed outlines of character and intent.

Following this, a publisher will usually ask for a full synopsis of the story so they can see exactly what the author intends to write, and so they can make editorial comments early on, thus preventing the problem of a major rewrite at a later stage. (One author was told by an editor that all editors dream of receiving a perfect book that needs no work done on it at all. An almost unknown phenomenon. Many editors seem to be inveterate tinkerers and thoroughly enjoy and want to justify their work.)

Synopses are not only of use to publishers. You will, by now, know that books in all age groups have quite tight word limits. It is taking a real chance for a writer to start a book for 11-year-olds without much idea of what is going to happen, but with the hope that whatever does happen will resolve itself exactly to the word limit. In other words, a professional author *has* to have a pretty good idea of where a piece of work is going, if only to make sure it gets to its conclusion at the right time and not 2,000 words short or 5,000 words over the acceptable length of the book.

Some authors sit down with a bottle of vodka and several packets of cigarettes and write until the story is all there in front of them. Some write thumbnail sketches then wander off for a while to let their ideas simmer and stew. Others use the 'tumble drier' approach, in which the plot is allowed to rumble around in their heads until it resolves itself.

Still others take a long walk to thrash out complicated plot lines. Others use the 'orienteering' approach, in which individual ideas are run up mental flagpoles in a more-or-less straight line from chapter 1 to chapter whatever; the task then being to map-read your way from flagpole to flagpole.

Then again, the plot may come to an author piecemeal and out of order, starting life as a heap of scraps which need to be sorted out before a coherent pattern emerges. A plot may start from a single observation which clicks with something that has been languishing in your Ideas File for months. Marry them up and see what happens.

A synopsis presented to a publisher is not written in stone, and plots can be altered as you progress when better ways forward present themselves. Do not be afraid to make radical changes if second thoughts turn out to be better thoughts. And be prepared to have to rewrite existing parts if a brilliant idea suddenly hits you halfway through a book but requires 'seeding' earlier on. (A computer, incidentally, makes this sort of rewriting a much simpler procedure. Worth remembering!)

Some authors accost their friends, family or partners and use them as sounding boards or alternative brains when plots are being devised. If you have no children of your own, then the children of a friend could prove an invaluable source of ideas. A couple of hours with a child can produce better results than six months of staring at a blank sheet of paper or screen.

Some authors like to keep their synopsizing to a minimum, simply sketching out the plot and leaving the details for the full writing process. Others will write formidably detailed, scene-by-scene, chapter-by-chapter outlines that leave nothing to the imagination, and which even include planned exchanges of dialogue and snippets of narrative.

The fact is that you must discover the plotting method which best suits you, but we emphasize that you must not be afraid of changing things in midstream if new thoughts occur. Very few authors really know exactly how they plan on getting from A to Z: after all, the journey is all part of the pleasure. We will cover this more fully in the next chapter, when we discuss plot structures.

Checklist

■ Target your market.

■ Make sure that your idea fits the niche into which you wish it to go.

■ Make sure the level of language and so on suits the age group for whom you are writing.

■ Similarly, make sure the length of the work is suitable for the market.

■ Do not include dialogue or material which is unsuited to the age group you are targeting.

■ Try to get into regular contact with children of the appropriate age.

■ Do not use transient slang.

■ Try to make your work as 'timeless' as possible.

- Aim for the average ability level of the age range for which you are writing.
- The age of your main characters should be at the top end of the intended reading age group.
- Be frugal with those adverbs and adjectives, and aim to keep the narrative bright, lucid and engaging.
- And, lest you forget, *enjoy yourself!*

5 | THE BASICS OF WRITING FICTION

You don't need to be a mechanic to drive a car.

Meaning what, exactly? Theatre critic Kenneth Tynan once remarked that a critic was a person who knew the way but could not drive.

Our point is that a good author can be a person who knows how to drive but has only the most basic knowledge of what actually goes on beneath the figurative bonnet of the English language. In other words, you do not need a Master's degree in English in order to be an innovative, successful and published author. Of course, you need to have an eye and an ear for language and an ability to present your personality on the page in an engaging way, but that does not necessarily mean you need to know why a pluperfect is a pluperfect, or why a phrase is not a sentence, or why the plural of 'foot' is not 'foots'. A highly academic knowledge of your language may help to produce polished work which, however grammatically perfect, may still bore the hind legs off an entire herd of elephants.

A good eye for words on paper and a highly-tuned ear for conversation will take you a lot further than years of technical tutelage. As long as you have mastered the basics of your language, you should become your own teacher and your classroom the world around you. An author, particularly of fiction, is selling his/her personality via the medium of the printed word. Your job is to make the ink and the paper or screen dissolve away from your reader and to leave only the pleasure of a well-told story.

Plot-line basics

It is widely said that there are only three basic plots in fiction, subdivided into seven classic plot lines derived probably from the

Greeks and later used by the likes of Shakespeare *et al*. We decided to track down a more definitive answer to this 'rumour' and ended up posing the question on the internet. Replies came back from all over the world, from university professors to librarians. Here are some of the responses:

1. Cinderella (rags to riches).

2. Faust (the debt has to be repaid).

3. Achilles (the fatal flaw).

4. The eternal triangle (man plus woman plus X).

5. The spider and the fly (good versus evil).

6. Romeo and Juliet – a tragedy (boy meets girl, boy loses girl, boy gets girl back).

7. The great 'romance' (X meets Y, they hate each other, they live happily ever after).

In addition to the seven traditional (movie) plots you could arguably now add an eighth: the indomitable hero (e.g. Terminator).

Boy murders girl, girl murders boy.

And let's not forget 'Boy meets whale ...'

Several of the respondents claimed that there are in fact 36 dramatic situations, and provided lists of these. One other thing which this exercise shows is just how useful and interesting the internet can be.

However many plots there may be, one publisher boiled the whole affair down to this: 'There is a problem. The problem develops. The problem is solved.' This is known as the 'beginning', the 'middle' and the 'end', without which story-telling ceases to function in any coherent way. What you do not want is for the beginning to drag on until about three-quarters of the way through the book, and for the middle and the end to get crammed into the final couple of chapters.

This may seem pretty obvious, but one agent told us of a manuscript they received in which the *actual* story did not get off the ground until the final chapter; the book seemed, in fact, to stop dead just as things were getting interesting, having wasted thousands of words on totally unnecessary introductions to a whole bunch of extraneous characters and events. Publishers and agents often receive manuscripts with 50-page introductions or very promising picture book stories which fall badly out of balance when the author tries to wrap the plot up in the final couple of paragraphs. This kind of thing happens when an inexperienced author dives head-first into writing a novel without giving much thought to where they are going with the story or why they are going there.

This can be avoided if you sit down and ask yourself a few salient questions before setting pen to paper (or digit to keyboard).

What do you want to say, and why do you want to say it?

A work of fiction must be inspired by *something*. Even if the idea seems to have sprung fully formed from the depths of your imagination, you can bet your life it has been gestating away in there.

By now you should have a well developed and fully functioning Ideas File. Having brilliant ideas, though, is only the first part. Next you need to get your brilliant ideas into some coherent form.

Story lengths

Remember what we told you about the way publishers approach their market? Books for young adults are generally longer than books for the 'middle fiction' range. These are, in turn, longer than story books, and story books are longer than picture books. In other words, if the characters or events you have come up with steer you towards a young adult audience (12+), you need to draw the plot out to cover about 40,000 words, or more. If your characters and the things they do better suit a 10–12-year-old audience then you are looking at approximately 30,000 words – and so on down the age range.

You may think that a length of 40,000 words gives ample scope for 'off the ball' episodes and character studies, but bear in mind that a 14-year-old is no more likely to appreciate being bored by long, dry, uneventful passages than is a 6-year-old. In longer books, plots may become more involved and convoluted, but always keep your 'average' reader in mind and never get carried away by whole chapters that will only confuse and frustrate a reader.

Plotting

Mystery is one thing, profound confusion quite another. It is perfectly acceptable to string a reader along with clues and red herrings, but in the end everything must make sense. The reader of a crime thriller or mystery story must be able to look back over the book once they have come to the denouement and wonder how they were so dumb as to not spot all the clues strewn across the preceding chapters.

Like one of those three-dimensional pictures, in which the image leaps out at you when you look at it in a particular way, a thriller, mystery or crime story must, in the end, have a clarity of plotting. (Of course there are books and films which do not seem to supply all the clues, or provide all of the answers, or may deliberately intend to be obscure. Whilst these may seek to provoke our imagination, they can also be tremendously frustrating and unsatisfying to many people.)

Murder/mystery/crime-type books need to be carefully thought out. For example, the usual method of plotting crime stories would be to start with the initial 'event' (murder, theft or other crime), then leapfrog to the 'resolution' before starting on the laborious process of working out how the two ends of the story are to be linked together.

A murder mystery

Professor X is found dead in her study with an axe embedded in her skull. That is your event; the purpose of your story is to discover who did the embedding and why.

Your 'hero' (or 'heroine') will be the person who unmasks the 'villain'. Your villain will be the murderer, who leads your hero a merry dance right up until the last page, when the hero turns, points an accusing finger and says 'That person did it, and I will now tell you how and why!'

Your hero need not be a genius, nor young, nor sighted; your hero could be an engaging affable, but slightly dim person who discovers the truth by accident whilst looking in entirely the wrong direction. Your heroine need not be a member of a police force, or from a police officer's family; she could be the caretaker's daughter, who saw something odd on the morning of the murder, but to whom no one will listen.

One of the problems with thrillers or crime stories where children or young people are the lead characters is that ingenious methods need to be thought up to explain why adults do not take over the whole investigation. A major part of your skill as a children's author of such plot-driven books will be to come up with plausible reasons why your protagonists do not (or fail to) tell any adults what is going on, and concocting events that are viable and reasonable in a world fraught with 'stranger dangers'.

Exercise 8

You are writing a detective novel. Your lead characters are a girl and a boy aged about 12. A theft has taken place at their school: the charity box has been raided.

The two youngsters have a pretty good idea who the thief is. Come up with thoughts on the following:

1. Who stole the money and why?
2. Why do the youngsters suspect the thief?
3. Why do they seek to solve the crime themselves rather than pass on the information to the authorities?

Here are some obvious answers:

1. The money was stolen by the headteacher to feed a secret gambling habit.
2. The youngsters saw the headteacher coming out of the room where the money was kept only a few minutes before the theft was reported.
3. They dare not tell anyone because who would believe the word of two students against that of their headteacher?

So as not to make things too easy for you, now come up with three different ways of setting up that plot *without* the headteacher being the villain.

What and why

Let us go back to the original questions of 'what' and 'why' for a moment.

What are you writing?

Has a fascinating character come to you? Someone whose life and adventures you are desperate to write about because the person in your head is so interesting? Archetypes have been Toad of Toad Hall from *The Wind in the Willows*. A. A. Milne's Piglet from the *Winnie the Pooh* stories. Long John Silver, Pippi Longstocking, Heidi and Anne of Green Gables. All of these characters are strong, rounded and well defined, but they all have something else in common: they are all attached to an interesting plot.

Interesting characters

You see, strong characters are not enough. They have to *do* things. They have to do *interesting* things that will hold the attention of a reader from page one. (We shall come back to the 'from page one' problem in a moment.)

Has an amazing adventure come to you when travelling or in a dream or while you were watching television? It could involve helicopters, frantic rescues from underground caverns or from spaceships careering into the heart of the sun. It could involve the protagonists in fearful perils and extraordinary split-second rescues from massive explosions, but even a plot stuffed to the rafters with action and thrills requires an additional element. It requires the reader to *care* about what happens to the people to whom all these amazing things are happening: if two people are skydiving with faulty parachutes, the reader has to want them not to hit the ground with a gigantic thud. Even the most thrilling, nail-biting plot needs to be peopled with characters whose safety and survival is of some concern to the reader.

If, as sometimes happens in plot-driven stories, the characters are a little two-dimensional, then they have to be placed in a situation where their actions are important on a wider scale. For example, animal rights warriors have released thousands of infected and mutated rates from a mad professor's lab. Battling Fred Cardboard and his team must recapture all the rates before they infect the whole population, causiing millions of lives to be lost. Battling Fred and his gang may be of relatively little importance in such a book, but their actions will be of vast importance to the reader if disaster is to be averted.

So, here are some basic equations:

Characters without a plot = a lot of aimless dithering about.
Plot without characters = plenty of action, no involvement.

Think of all those 'disaster' movies in which you have paid to see a major catastrophe and lots of spectacular special effects. First, though, you will be introduced to the characters whom the disaster is going to affect. The more you care and believe in those victims, the greater your (albeit temporary) emotional involvement.

Far too many scripts arrive on publishers' and agents' desks in which the covering letter points out that the enclosed novel has 'something for everyone'. Wrong! For 'something for everyone' read 'written in a totally unfocused way and probably completely unmarketable'.

Different approaches

Different types of fiction require different approaches. For instance, a thriller should end most chapters with a cliff-hanger, so that the reader is desperate to find out what happens next. A character-led book should have chapters that end with some dilemma facing one or other of the characters, again so that the reader is forced to start a new chapter in order to find out how the problem is resolved.

Short chapters are generally a good idea. A reader may see a five-page chapter and think, 'I'll just read *one* more chapter before I put the light out', whereas they would put the book down for the day if they saw that the next chapter was 25 pages long. Psychologically, bite-size chapters can easily draw a reader into reading much more than the few pages they intended.

Dialogue has the effect of breaking the page up and of avoiding big blocks of narrative. Have your characters do most of the talking, if possible, and limit your narrative asides to scene-setting and to important explanations.

Chapters do not need to be of a uniform length (but their lengths should not vary too wildly). A chapter needs to encompass a scene or series of interlinked scenes which have some basic concession and, as we said above, they should end at a point which leaves things unresolved. The *next* chapter should end with a vital point unexplained so that the reader just has to start reading the following chapter, and so on right through the book.

If your book follows several characters all doing different, perilous things at the same time, you could leave a character hanging off a cliff for entire chapters whilst you show what someone else is up to. Then you can drop a piano out of a window beneath which *another* character is standing and finally go back to see how the first character hanging off the cliff is getting on! Short of applying strong glue to the outer book covers, this is the best way of creating something that is clumsily and awkwardly referred to as 'unputdownable'.

Why are you writing this story?

Presumably you have an idea or a series of ideas in which you think other people will be fascinated. Inside your head, these ideas may well be totally stunning, but the test of your writing skills will be how well you can present these ideas to your audience. As with most things, first impressions are vital. Most agents and publishers will tell you that they can spot a 'winner' within the first paragraph or, at worst, within the first three pages.

So, how do you kindle their enthusiasm?

In a work of fiction you will need to introduce your characters, put them in some sort of context, and give some inkling to the reader of what sort of book this is going to be. However, you cannot hope to achieve all of these things on the first page. Page one needs to involve something that will grab your reader by the lapels and absolutely *demand* that he or she carries on reading. Most of your background detail can be sketched in a few pages later.

For instance, the book can open with a knock on a door. The door is opened. The dialogue makes it clear that the person inside the house knows the visitor but is shocked by them turning up so unexpectedly.

The first chapter can then continue by describing the reaction of the various people inside the house to the new arrival; and during these exchanges the relationships of the various people can become clear. The chapter can end with a decision having been made as to whether the visitor is allowed to stay in the house or is thrown out again. (The unexpected visitor could be an errant teenager returning to the family home after an unexplained absence of several days/weeks/months.)

With the situation and the main characters now firmly in place, the second chapter could take a reflective look back at how the situation came into being.

Start with a bang

Start your book with a bang, and explain the reason for the bang later on. Look at how action/thriller films get into gear. (Observing how a well-written, popular film is put together is just as relevant as dissecting books.) Very often such films start off with the main character involved in some unexplained action. In *Raiders of the Lost Ark*, the entire opening scene actually has very little relevance to the main plot, but does an excellent job of introducing Indiana Jones and explaining his rivalry with the French archaeologist who is later to become his most potent enemy. Similarly, watching the last few minutes of television soap operas can show you how to construct breath-taking cliff-hangers.

In your book, explanations for who is so-and-so can wait. Explanations for why so-and-so is doing something can wait. Just have them get on with it. If the action is gripping, the reader will be prepared to wait a while to find out more on who, what, why and where.

It is not always necessary to set the scene before the action starts, and in a lot of cases, it is far better to leave the explanations until later. If the plot centres on one climactic scene, then maybe a flash-forward could be used as a teaser. For a book involving an earthquake, you could always preface the start of the book with a few pages describing the first few minutes of the quake, before going back into real time and covering the days leading up to the quake.

(Flashbacks can serve a similar function as flash-forwards. The book could start with the seventeenth-century burning of a witch, then fast-forward to the present day and the lives of people living in the same village, and how the echoes of that ancient event affects their lives.)

Look at the opening lines of some classic, best-selling or modern children's novels. Do you want to read on?

Exercise 9

Write the opening paragraph for a book.

Your first line could probably be more interesting than 'Once upon a time' or 'It was a dark and stormy night'. Something tantalizing might include:

- (For a picture book.) The duck crashed through the window and landed in Gemma's breakfast cereal.

- (For middle fiction.) On his way home from school one day, Raymond was picked up and carried off by a gigantic space ship displaying learner driver plates.

- (For young adult fiction.) Mum was always saying, 'Wear clean underwear. You never know when you might get hit by a bus.' As I lay on the hospital trolley, I didn't know which worried me more: Mum, my underwear or the bus.

Question your motives

Why are you are seeking to get your work published? Do you have an overwhelming urge to entertain people? Do you want to share some information or knowledge, or do you simply want to be rich and famous?

Perhaps you have an idea for a series or sequence of books. To be honest, your chances of hitting on a perfect idea or formula without a lot of experience and research are pretty limited. You may have read one book of a successful series and thought to yourself, 'I could do that'. Too late! Someone else has already done it. There is no point in labouring long and hard to reinvent the wheel. You need to come up with an entirely *new* idea, and it will have to include a formula with the potential to run and run. Similarly, it is no good having a great idea for a six-book series which peters out after two or three books because you have explored every possible area of interest.

The step from being an aspiring writer to being the author of a successful series, is like going from having a short walk to running a marathon in the Olympics. Never discard those brilliant series ideas – just be prepared to be patient. Few publishers are likely to commission an unknown author to produce a series, but the situation may well be very different for an author with a few published works under his/her belt.

What other motives could you have? Maybe you are trying to work your way through some personal problems via the printed word; maybe you have an autobiographical tale to tell; or maybe you have a moral point to make. All well and good, so long as the end-product is *entertaining*. Tales of personal angst, no matter how universal the cause, still need to be 'page turners' (and you need to remember that publishers have their own motives and criteria). Here are some of the questions which may run through a commissioning editor's mind once they have read your story:

- Will it be profitable/inexpensive to produce?
- Will it sell?
- Is it complementary to our list?
- Do I have a slot for it in my publishing schedule?
- What do I think of the work?
- Is it a new approach to a subject?
- Is it of value and worthy of being published?
- Who is the author, and what are they like?
- What are the views of the editorial, sales and marketing departments?

The above may not necessarily be the best criteria in the world to use as a basis for starting a piece of work, but the points do give you an idea of the thought processes of publishers.

Something else to consider is the constantly shifting fashion within the book industry. A topic which publishers may be falling over themselves to purchase one year may be totally passé two years later. Part of being a successful author is the ability to maintain that vital balance between the personal and the professional. Write what has meaning for you, but keep one eye on the marketplace.

Finding a voice

(Here we go again: something which seems totally straightforward at first glance turns out to be anything but!) Is your book going to be written in the first person, or the third person? Is it going to use past tense or present tense? Is it going to include the thought processes of your characters and, if so, how many minds are you planning on giving the reader access to?

We shall deal with these dilemmas one at a time.

First person

First person is where the entire story is narrated by one (or more) of the characters in the book – usually a single, dominant character. In this format, the voice of the author is subordinated to that of the lead character. *Everything* in the book must be written in the voice of the chosen character. All the events in the story must be filtered through the mind and voice of this character.

Obviously, a strong, well thought-out and rounded character is needed for this technique to work. Similarly, the author of a first-person book has to shade and colour the narration so that it comes across as being within the purview of the age and experience expectations of the speaking character. A 10-year-old narrator will have a different version of a series of events than a narrator aged 8 or 16 would.

In a broader context, consider how horseplay between some 10-year-old children which results in a valuable vase being broken will be viewed by the children themselves, and then by the adult who owns the vase, hears the crash and comes to investigate. Try writing this scene in the first person, initially from the child's point of view, and then from an adult perspective.

Here is a start for you:

Child: We were only *playing*. I mean, a person is entitled to *play*, aren't they? And if that vase is so totally *priceless* then Mum was a bit daft to leave it standing there in the first place ...

Adult: I've told and told you until I'm blue in the face: don't horse around in the living room, you might break something! So you can imagine how I felt when I heard that crash! I just *knew* what had happened.

Can you add a third voice, that of an older brother or sister who has been left in charge of the children? How would that person react to the breakage?

A problem with writing in the first person is that it can be a little tricky to include information which is vital for the plot, but which the narrator does not know. In first-person stories, the reader knows only what the narrator relates (although devices such as, 'I didn't know this until later, but what happened was ...', can help out in some cases). Another problem occurs when the story involves several different characters all doing different things. The reader can only learn what has been going on via the narrator being told by these characters. To solve such problems, it is usually preferable for events to be recounted in the narrator's presence, so that information is passed on in a conversational form, rather than leaving your narrator to regurgitate information in large, hard-to-digest blocks of prose.

However, it is possible for a first-person book to be narrated by someone who is not directly involved in the action: 'I'd like to tell you about something that happened to some friends of mine ...' In this format, a coherent but uninvolved overview can be constructed in which the opinion of the narrator may not coincide with the opinions of other characters in the book. The courting activities and rituals of a bunch of 13-year-old girls and boys could be amusingly narrated by a younger sister or brother of one of the protagonists: 'Don' t ask me what my 13-year-old big brother Matthew sees in her, but he's started getting really stupid over the girl who delivers our morning newspaper.' The benefit of this format is that it 'personalizes' a story. The narrator 'speaks' directly to the reader, rather than through the imposed voice of the author. Thus the narrator becomes the reader's 'friend' in a more immediate way, and if it works well, the reader will feel as if they are having the story related to them in much the same way as friends tell each other stories in the playground.

Third person

The third-person format is where the narrator of the story is separated from the action, and the word 'I' does not appear except in dialogue. The reader is one step removed from the characters in the book, whose activities are related by a 'storyteller'. This kind of story-telling goes back into the days of oral mythology, when poets and bards would chronicle the activities of the gods and the immortals for their audience. The third-person format is useful when a story involves a lot of contemporaneous activity and when the narrative needs to shift constantly from one set of characters to another. It is easy to switch from perspective to perspective in a third-person narrative. For example, one character could be held at gunpoint by the villain of the story while the other characters could be searching for him or her. The third-person format allows the narrative to shift its perspective rapidly from character to character and event to event in a way that would be much more difficult if the book were written in the first person.

Third-person narratives also allow for an element of authorial intervention. A character being chased across moors by a maniac will hardly have time to look around them and describe their environment. But within such an urgent setting, the author through the third-person narrator, will be able to snatch a few moments to describe the scene, and perhaps even to give a voice to the maniac. In some cases it may be vital for the reader to know the reason behind the chase, even though the character being chased does not. This style allows the author to tell the readers things which the leading characters in the book may not know. In a suspense thriller, it adds a lot of tension if the reader knows there is a dangerous maniac in the closet which an oblivious lead character is about to open.

The problem with the third-person format is that it can separate the reader from the characters, although it is perfectly permissible for a third-person narrated book to include the private thoughts of as many characters as the author should choose. Presenting the 'thoughts' of a character can be a useful device, but you need to be careful over exactly how many brains to include to which the reader is allowed access. It will not take long for the reader to work out who the villain is in a 'whodunit' story if they learn the thoughts of all the characters, or all characters bar one. It is usually best to limit reader's access to one or two lead characters, and use the 'thinking' device only when there is no one to whom the character can vocalize their reactions. Dialogue is always more lively than narrative, so when using the third-person format, be sure to allow your characters to 'talk' the plot along as much as possible.

The advantage of the third person is that the author is able to narrate events in their 'own' voice (or in the voice of a disinterested and unbiased third party). It allows for the motives of several different characters to be explored without prejudice and for a number of simultaneous plot strands to be followed simply by dint of the narrator scene-hopping in a way that a first-person narrator would find very difficult.

Exercise 10

Try writing the scene with the broken vase again, this time in the third person. Write it first in the context of a children's book and, therefore, from a child's view, and then from an adult perspective. The two versions should come out quite differently. Explore the differences and think about what you have learnt from this exercise.

Multiple narratives

You can write a book narrated by two or more first-person characters. A simple device for this sort of story-telling is for successive chapters to be headed with the name of the character whose voice is being heard. In this way, you could describe a romance between two teenagers and how characters react to the same events with no authorial overview at all. An evening at the movies for Simon and Helen might be seen as a great success by Simon. He may tell the reader what a great time he had, how he held Helen's hand all through the movie and how he is looking forward to their next date. Helen might have a totally different story to tell. She might tell the reader how utterly bored she was, point out that Simon wore aftershave which was overpowering and had clammy hands, and make it quite clear that she has no intention of ever dating Simon again. Successive chapters could then chronicle the 'romance' from those two sides, with neither of the characters actually having much idea of what is going through the mind of the other while the reader knows *everything*. How might the story be enlivened? What if Helen gradually realizes her first impressions were wrong and that she really likes Simon after all? And what if Simon, dejected by Helen's rejections of his advances, decides she is not worth the effort and stops asking her out on the very day that Helen decides she will finally agree to a date? Such a story could, of course, easily be written in the third person, but think how much more lively and immediate it becomes when the only voices being heard are those of Simon and Helen.

A favourite first-person format, by the way, is the *diary*. A number of very successful books have been written in this style, so you would be expected to come up with something new to awaken the average publisher's interest. A particular problem with telling a story in diary format is that it is virtually impossible for events to be given anything other than a very immediate perspective. The writer of a diary is not going to be in a position to explain events of immediate relevance if the explanation does not occur for a few more days. In some types of story it does no harm for the reader to know only what the narrator knows; in others, this lack of an overview, or at least of hindsight, will make the story virtually impossible to convey coherently.

A story can also be written so that it alternates between the third person and the first person. One way of doing this is by the inclusion of letters from one character to another within the general third-person framework. This can help to present the opinions and attitudes of a particular character in a way that would otherwise be less vivid. Returning to the Helen and Simon story, the date could be described in the third person and without any particular insight into how the two characters felt. This could be followed up by Helen writing a letter to a girl pen-friend, describing her feelings, and Simon to a friend, telling him how it all went (or at least how he thought it went). The story could even be given a further twist: Helen could be writing to a male pen-friend, in which case the reader will have to decide whether the things that Helen writes describe how she really feels or only how she wants her pen-friend to think she feels. Alternatively, how about writing the story so that the reader only thinks the letters were written by Helen, because they had her name at the bottom, but finds out later on that they were not written by Helen, but by Simon for his own entertainment, and were his assumptions of how Helen might be feeling!

By now you should be realizing that giving a book a voice and format is a complex and open-ended task – much like everything else in the writing world.

Books can also include time shifts. For instance, the first chapter could be set in the present day, but the second goes back six months to follow a different plot strand, or to explain how the present-day plot strand came about. In this manner, the entire book could time-hop through its story.

Non-human voices

Up until now, we have really been discussing formats for different *human* voices. Yet it is possible to write books in voices that are not human. Here are two obvious examples.

Aliens

You might choose to write a story from the perspective of a creature from another planet. If your chosen creature is a messy green blob from Mars, then you may have difficulty in rounding out the character (no pun intended!). Something reasonably humanoid or at least with a reasonably human attitude may allow for a whole sequence of amusing incidents based on misunderstandings between species. An alien race may land on earth whose method of communicating is via hitting each other over the heads with saucepans. How would this go down among humans?

The silvery spaceship comes to ground in the park and a door panel slides silently open. A being appears, clutching a saucepan. The creature proceeds to spell out 'Hello, how are you, my name is Ftunnng' by beating a rapid tattoo on the head of the leader of the welcoming committee with the saucepan.

A word of warning: success in this format is very difficult to achieve.

Animals

Anthropomorphism means giving animals human thoughts, motives and rationalities. This is a format to which you must give serious thought before embarking on any work. Unless you are planning on turning yourself into an animal, you are going to have to stretch your imagination to its limits if you are going to present a book in a first-person animal voice. Really, it is best not to try.

Several very successful books have been written in the third person, chronicling the adventures and activities of animals or groups of animals. *Watership Down* is one such title that immediately springs to mind. Richard Adams did an enormous amount of research work on the way rabbits behave in real life in order to give his book a semblance of 'reality'. He had to humanize the thinking processes of these animals, but their day-to-day lives were depicted in the same way as an average rabbit's. (As an aside, the other classic tale about this famous book is the number of times it was turned down by publishers before finally finding a home.)

Animals in clothes are not winners. Animals that live in houses, drive cars or play golf are not winners. The fact that you may be able to cite several books in which animals do exactly those things is irrelevant. Trust us, publishers do not look kindly on books where animals are just furry, hairy, spiky or scaly humans. A clever, well-written animal story can be a real winner, but have a good look around the marketplace to assess the competition before you get to work.

Whilst we are on the subject of non-human voices, there is one area in which we received an almost universal shriek of horror from all the publishers whom we contacted: investing inanimate objects with sentience, emotions, self-propelled movement and voices. True, there have been some notable successes in this field, but generally publishers will run a mile when confronted by Fiona the Friendly Frankfurter or Terrance the Talking Turtle. The following titles are from a list of stories submitted to a publisher and, to make things worse, handwritten on lined paper torn from a shorthand notebook:

- Mr Fudget the Toy Fixer
- Greg the Gnome
- Simon the Sea Gull
- Carly the Cat
- Bluey the Budgie
- Charlie the Chimney
- Betty in Bunnytown
- Violet the Vacuum Cleaner

Need we go on? The recipient editor probably read no more than the first page of 'Mr Fudget' before reaching for a rejection slip. One final thought on the talking animals front: on the whole, animals talking to each other is fine; animals talking to humans is not, unless handled with a great deal of skill.

The use of tense

Past tense, present tense and future tense. Yes, yet more ways to format that story of yours.

Past and present tense

The past tense is the usual way in which to tell a story.

> He ran across the road. She followed him, dodging the traffic as she tried to keep him in sight.

Effectively, the storyteller is relating a series of events which have already taken place, and putting them in that context by using past tense.

People will fall naturally into using the past tense when relaying anecdotes, although in some cases, a kind of urgency or immediacy can be maintained by the use of the present tense:

'So I say to him, I say, you come one step closer to me with that gherkin, and I'll have the law on you, so help me, I will. And he looks at me with his eyes all kind of narrowed-up, and I think: he's going to do it. And then he comes for me, and I run down the street, yelling my head off, and he chases me, waving his gherkin and shouting, stop! Stop!!'

Or,

'So I'm saying to him, I'm saying, you come one step closer to me with that gherkin, and I'll have the law on you, so help me, I will. And he's looking at me with his eyes all kind of narrowed-up, and I'm thinking: he's going to do it. And then he's coming for me, and I'm running down the street, yelling my head off, and he's chasing me, waving his gherkin and shouting, stop! Stop!!'

Now let us try it again in the past tense:

'So I said to him, I said, you come one step closer to me with that gherkin, and I'll have the law on you, so help me, I will. And he looked at me with his eyes all kind of narrowed-up, and I thought: he's going to do it. And then he came for me, and I ran down the street, yelling my head off, and he chased me, waving his gherkin and shouting, stop! Stop!!'

Or a different sort of past tense:

'So I was saying to him, I was saying, you come one step closer to me with that gherkin, and I'll have the law on you, so help me, I will. And he was looking at me with his eyes all kind of narrowed-up, and I was thinking: he's going to do it. And then he was coming for me, and I was running down the street, yelling my head off, and he was chasing me, waving his gherkin and shouting, stop! Stop!!'

So you can see how both present and past tenses can be used in different ways to create different effects. And that is not only true for first-person narratives:

'You come one step closer to me with that gherkin,' she said, 'and I'll have the law on you, so help me I will.'

He looked at her with narrowed eyes and she realized he was about to pounce.

> She ran down the street, yelling for help while he chased after her, brandishing the deadly gherkin and shouting, 'Stop! Stop!!'

Present tense:

> 'You come one step closer to me with that gherkin,' she says, 'and I'll have the law on you, so help me I will.'

> He looks at her with narrowed eyes and she realizes he is about to pounce.

> She runs down the street, yelling for help while he chases after her, brandishing the deadly gherkin and shouting, 'Stop! Stop!!'

Using present tense cranks up the urgency of the piece. It creates the illusion that the reader is actually there while the event is taking place.

The big problem with using present tense is that it is a little unnatural, and requires a good deal of concentration to make sure you do not find yourself slipping back into the much more comfortable use of past tense.

Present tense has an urgency which leads to plot limitations, especially in connection with first-person present tense. Not only does the reader not know anything that the narrator does not know, but there is absolutely no way of covering simultaneous action by other characters or clarifying complexities.

Enough about gherkins!

Exercise 11

Using the above examples as guidelines, write a page-long piece in past tense on any topic you choose, and then rewrite it using the present tense. Make a note of how the use of different tenses alters the story.

List a few examples of the sort of stories that you think would work best in past tense, and those that would benefit from the immediacy of present tense.

Dialogue

Consider the following:

> Picture a scene of rolling countryside. A man and a woman stand on the brow of a hill. It is a block-busting generation-spanning tale of love, revenge, money, hatred, money, wealth, power and money, but not necessarily in that order, written by someone called Sapphire Diamond or Jack Ironstone.
>
> A rider approaches on a black stallion. The woman speaks.
>
> 'Oh! Can it be?' Elvira gasped breathlessly. 'Yes, it's Tyler, my adopted half-brother whom Father found in the gutter and brought home to share our good fortune despite what the old gypsy woman said about him being a black-hearted devil. But why is he here? Father sent him to manage the New York office of our multi-national kippering firm and not to return unless something terrible happened. I have not had word from him these past two years, although we were loving playmates as children and in my innocence I always thought we would be married one day.'

No problems about knowing who Tyler is. And, as exaggerated as that speech may be, it covers a common problem with dialogue: translating conversations into readable and realistic dialogue on the page.

How do people speak to one another? To unravel this riddle you will need to take yourself off for yet another stint of dialogue research. Go somewhere you will be able to overhear people talking to one another. Listen to how they speak and try to analyse what is going on. This could be a party, meeting or anywhere two or more people are gathered in conversation.

Poor dialogue will let a good story down badly. We need to stress how important it is that you get it right. There is a profound difference between real conversations and conversations as they appear on television or in books. In real life, people will start a sentence, then change tack suddenly, stammer over certain words, repeat themselves, digress, stop midway through saying one thing to say something completely different, leave observations hanging in mid-air, half-say things, contradict themselves and talk over one another until language seems to turn into some kind of wildly stirred minestrone soup of sounds, sense and nonsense, meaning and meaninglessness.

Authors have tried to recreate this maelstrom of 'real' conversation on the page, but on the whole it is the job of an author to make sense of dialogue rather than simply to mirror it on paper.

On the other hand, to pull dialogue too far from its natural origins creates its own problems. 'Real' conversation may be incomprehensible, but obviously 'made-up' conversation is no better. A reader has to believe in the characters you invent, and a major part of that belief hinges on your ability to make those characters speak in a natural and unaffected way.

A good rule of thumb is to speak dialogue aloud. Your family and friends may think you have lost your senses when they hear you arguing with yourself behind closed doors, but the fact is that the only way to check whether a line of dialogue or an exchange between characters really 'works' is to hear it spoken aloud or acted out.

As stressed in the last chapter, avoid using the fleeting idioms of the present day. You want your book to be read in 20 years' time, so unless the plot has to be anchored in a particular time-frame, you will want your characters to sound fresh and contemporary to future audiences. Street slang should largely be avoided. In real life, a person may say 'Know what I mean?' at the end of every utterance, but on paper this affectation will rapidly become irritating to the reader, and the irritation will be aimed at the author, not at the character.

An aggressive person picking a fight may repeat the same bullet-hard phrase over and over to gain attention. 'You talking to me? You talking to me? You talking to me? You talking to me?' Children will often swear for no particular reason and without aggression, simply because such words are considered a normal part of 'playground' conversation amongst their friends. Swearing and bad language are not automatically removed from books for young adults (although they would obviously be inappropriate for younger age groups), but you should think carefully before having one teenager character tell another to 'get lost' in expletives. This has little to do with the moral standards of publishers and editors, and plenty to do with selling books: adults do not necessarily want less socially acceptable language to be seen to be authorized by having it presented to their children in the pages of a book. If you want to write a down-to-earth, nitty-gritty, urban-realism type book filled with drug fiends, teenage thieves and social outcasts, by all means do so – but be prepared for the fall-out and do not be surprised if few publishers show any desire to take it on.

A real conversation does to grammar, syntax and language what a 1-kilogram club hammer does to a pane of glass. It smashes it into fragments. Your job is to pick up the pieces, discard what is unnecessary, realign what is pertinent, and reconstruct seamlessly what is left. In real life most conversation is of little long-term relevance. Much of it is anecdotal: explaining the day's events to a friend or partner; retelling an amusing incident or an outrageous one; repeating a tale told by a work colleague or schoolfriend; asking for the salt to be passed; enquiring when dinner will be ready or where a fresh shirt is to be found. You know the sort of conversation we mean. Vital as such interaction is in real life, it should not intrude into written dialogue, unless possibly you are trying to show the reader that a character is having a totally boring evening – and even then it should be done very briefly. No one wants to read pages of irrelevant dialogue.

All dialogue has one of two possible purposes: either it is there to move the plot along, or it is there to deepen the understanding of the characters who are speaking and their relationship to one another. Thus, *keep dialogue short and keep it to the point*.

At the same time, bear in mind when you are putting conversations down in print that different people express themselves in different ways. A shy person, for example, with important information to convey will express themselves in a different way from someone with a loud, outgoing personality. A single character will use several different modes of speech depending upon their audience.

How you are going to frame your dialogue? Is anything wrong with the following?

Jeanette came running into the room.

'I've seen him!' she gasped breathlessly.

'Who?' Sasha enquired excitedly, leaping up.

'Alvin Knockersbury!' exclaimed Jeanette impatiently.

'What?' Gladys broke in urgently. '*The* Alvin Knockersbury? The pop star?' Her face was alive with excitement.

'Exactly!' Jeanette said sighingly. 'Alvin Knockersbury. My hero!'

'I like him better than you do!' wailed Sasha groaningly. 'And now I'm going to miss him because Mum won't let me go out.'

'Your mum won't know if you sneak out,' Gladys said whisperingly. 'Who's to tell her?'

'Him!' Sasha complained despairingly, pointing to the 20-stone guard who clutched the other end of the chain which her mother had attached to her ankle.

'Don't worry about me,' the guard said smilingly. 'I'm Alvin Knockersbury's biggest fan.'

'Hoorah!' Jeanette whooped exultantly. 'Now we can all go and see Alvin!'

And without further ado the four of them raced pantingly for the door.

This is what is known in the trade as 'adverbitis'. It is a similar disease to 'adjectivitis'. The chief symptom is an author's chronic inability to leave nouns or verbs alone. Why write 'she said' when you could embroider your text with 'sadly' or 'gladly' or 'effusively'? Why use 'said' when you could put 'exclaimed', 'ranted', 'quipped', 'declared', 'opined', 'effused' or 'remarked'? All of these words are perfectly acceptable in moderation: if someone makes an exclamation, then by all means say so; or if a person is breathless, then do not hesitate to mention it. However, these words need to be used sparingly and with caution, otherwise the dialogue becomes overburdened and loses all resonance. Bad dialogue can make even a hardened editor cringe, and the overuse of adverbs serves only to make the author's confidence in their work seem rather limited.

Keep interjections between dialogue to a minimum. There is nothing wrong with a simple 'he said' and 'she said', and if the dialogue is between two people and relatively straightforward, you could even leave the speech entirely to its own devices and give only a guiding 'she said' and 'he said' here and there as reference points. Be careful if you have three or more characters in conversation: a reader can quickly lose track of what is going on if the author does not reference each comment back to its source. It is no good if, halfway down a long tract of dialogue, a reader has to count his/her way back to the top of the page in order to figure out who is saying what.

On the subject of dialogue between several characters, you should try to ensure that, if there are four people present, each of them gets a word in every so often, even if it means sharing dialogue around more than is usual. A reader cannot see a character who is not mentioned or who does not talk. If a character in a scene neither speaks nor does anything, you would be as well to ask yourself whether that person really needs to be there at all. This is especially pertinent when you have a 'gang' who all meet together. Ensure in any ensemble scenes that everyone gets at least one line to say.

Sharing dialogue around has an additional function, especially in stories that require set-piece explanations (such as a mystery story or a crime thriller). What could become a tedious monologue by one character can be greatly enlivened if shared between two or three, more so if the narrative thread of the explanation or exposition is drawn out by a character who asks questions. There is a story-telling rationale behind Batman being teamed with Robin, Sherlock Holmes hanging out with Dr Watson, and Dr Who's succession of travelling companions. They are there, at least in part, to draw out explanations and to break up what would otherwise become boring soliloquies.

Another problem with dialogue can occur when an author is very obviously out of touch with young people and the way they express themselves. Should you not have regular contact with the age group for whom you are writing, you must find some means of occasional access or, at worst, take to watching children's television. The latter is not the perfect solution to the problem, because it means you are only hearing edited and regurgitated dialogue rather than going to the source – but in the early days it will give you an idea of how professional authors approach their craft and it will furnish you with many useful pointers. In the end, though, you ought to be shaping your dialogue and your characters from the world around you, and not through the filter of fellow authors.

Exercise 12

Rewrite the exchange about Alvin Knockersbury with an eye to removing the excess adverbs and adjectives. As with the examples of the Lord Byron biography, retain the meaning and interest of the piece whilst jettisoning all the rest.

Once you have 'weeded' the exchange, you could pause here to practise on dialogue of your own. It is probably sensible to restrict yourself to two characters for the moment (you can worry about convincingly written crowd scenes later on). Set up a scene where two characters are having an argument, pick your own topic, and give the two characters totally opposing points of view. Write a page-long piece of dialogue.

Use only the word 'said' when you are indicating who is speaking. No 'retorts' or 'declareds' or 'proclaimeds'; use just plain old 'saids'. If you can, do not even put 'she said' every time one of the characters speaks. (But remember, never let a reader lose track of who is speaking.)

Read the conversation aloud to yourself. Could a real person actually have said the words you have put into your characters' mouths? Is the sentence structure correct, or would a person run out of breath half-way through? If you have a tape recorder, use it to listen back to your dialogue. Does it sound realistic? Can you believe that real people would say such things? If not, why not? Where are you going wrong? Does your dialogue come across as being too heavily written? Does it sound like it comes from a page rather than straight out of a human's mouth?

Once you feel comfortable with your page of dialogue, push yourself a little further by placing two characters in a different situation so that you have to take account of their surroundings as they speak. They could be walking along a street, hurrying through a busy park or out shopping together. Try to incorporate their movements into an unobtrusive, sympathetic narrative as they argue.

Now take the whole piece to another level by adding a third character with yet another point of view. Add a parent who tells the two children to stop arguing. Include the reaction of the children to this interruption. Add a younger child. Add several more characters. See what effect these people have on the argument.

The aim of this exercise (and all the other exercises in this book) is to take you one step closer to that point where, like the novice dancer who suddenly realizes she has stopped counting out the rhythm, you find your invented characters wresting the pen out of your hand and speaking with their own voices.

Grammar

We have mentioned the importance of having a good working knowledge of the grammar of the language in which you are writing. To extend this, you should know some of the common grammatical errors which drive publishers to distraction.

Apostrophes cause people an awful lot of trouble. Its? It's? Its'? It is pretty straightforward, and you really ought to try and remember it:

It's is short for *'It is'*: 'It's time you went home.'

Its without the apostrophe is used when you want to say something like 'The boat skimmed the waves, its sails billowing in the wind.' *Its* refers back to the preceding direct object to denote the noun's possession of the following noun: 'the sails of it [the boat] billowing in the wind'.

Its' does not exist at all (although that fact does not stop people sticking their apostrophes in the strangest places).

Do'nt. No! No! No! It is *don't*, a contraction of *do not*. The apostrophe in this case denotes a missing letter, 'o'.

Can't: same thing – a contraction of cannot.

Likewise *shan't* (shall not), *won't* (will not), *isn't* (is not) and so on.

Also be careful when using apostrophes with plurals:

'Children's books' (books of the children): the plural, children does not end in *s*, therefore the apostrophe appears before the *s* denoting 'of the'.

The boy's book: one boy, owning one book.

The boys' book. More than one boy, collectively owning one book. The apostrophe appears after the *s*, thereby showing that the book belongs to more than one boy.

Something else to watch out for is dated or archaic language. Whatever time period your story is set in, you are writing for children of today. Phrases such as 'For he thought he was right' and 'Andrew was one of those people for whom dancing was easy' read as if the author is trying to impress the reader with his antiquated language prowess.

Beginning, middle and end

We have talked before about the importance of balancing your story across the three areas of plotting. You have to get the reader hooked by a particularly brilliant opening chapter, then ease the pace a little to fill in the background and put the characters and the action in an understandable context. Naturally you have plotted out a series of events through which your story will probably pass on its way to the final chapter.

We included 'probably' in that last sentence on purpose, as it is quite likely that when you get down to writing the full version of your story, you will find that things change in ways you could not have foreseen. As we said before, this is perfectly okay. If the story is taking you off into unexpected places, be prepared to go with the flow, so long as that flow does not take you up a blind alley. Keep your planned finale in mind. Perhaps the book is telling you that there is a better way to achieve your end than the one you originally intended.

Here are two different ways of presenting a story.

The surprise ending

Also known as the 'twist' or the 'sting', the surprise ending makes the reader follow the characters through a series of events without knowing how things are going to end. Will they all survive? Will someone die? Who? How? When?

In stories of this type, the tension and interest is maintained by adding unexpected twists in the tail of the plot, false endings, shocks and astonishing last-page revelations.

Note when writing this sort of story that it is not acceptable for all the murders to have been perpetrated by Oscar's younger half-sister who has lived all her life in Ulan Batur and whose existence is never mentioned until the detective drags her from a hiding place behind the potted palm. If you are planning great revelations, you must foreshadow them in some way. It is your job to put plenty of clues as to the existence of Oscar's half-sister, otherwise the reader feels cheated and it looks suspiciously like you made her up at the last minute because you could not think of anything better.

Clues and 'hooks' need to be carefully thought out and skilfully seeded throughout the story. The 'hook' is the means by which the 'hero' escapes certain death. An author needs to insert the 'hook' into the narrative in such a way that the reader is aware of its existence, but unaware of how important it will become later on.

An example

Somewhere earlier in your book, in a seemingly plot-irrelevant character exploring an off-the-ball scene, you show that Dirk Sox (a 17-year-old on work experience with an investigation agency) has considerable skill with a rope. Maybe you do not actually mention him lassoing things; maybe someone mentions it in passing. (In a narrative section in a book, it could be shown entirely in passing that Dirk's mum's mantelpiece is full of Golden Rope awards.)

Anyway, Dirk gets himself tangled up in a big international diamond-smuggling conspiracy and, towards the end of the book, is set adrift in a boat only 50 metres away from the edge of a 200-metre high waterfall towards which the rushing, churning waters are inexorably drawing him to his certain doom.

Previously, you will need to have mentioned, again in passing, that there is a length of rope in the boat. A long mooring rope, maybe? Perhaps the villains who cast Dirk adrift threw the mooring rope in his face as the boat floated away from the jetty.

Now you need one final 'hook' in the shape of a tree stump, pointed hunk of rock or some other geographical feature at the very lip of the waterfall.

(One amazing escape coming up!)

Dirk Sox grabs the rope. He fashions a lasso. He hurls the lasso at the tree stump. It misses! Arrgh! He has time for one final throw before plunging to his death. The lasso catches on the stump just as the boat careers over the edge of the waterfall. Dirk swings through the waterfall on the end of his rope. He is saved!

Why stop there? Why not include a map of where the diamonds are hidden. A vague map which says the diamonds are 'under water'? Dirk swings right through the waterfall on the end of his rope and finds himself in a secret cavern *behind* the waterfall. And in the secret cavern he finds the lost jewels! He has not only saved himself from certain death, but he has solved the mystery of the cryptic clue.

The trick when coming up with death-defying escapes is to have made the reader aware in advance of potential escape devices without being blatantly obvious about it.

Hooks are relevant not only to adventures: all plots need their share of clues and hooks if the climax is to be credibly explained.

The known ending

Another way of writing a book is to let the reader know from the beginning, exactly what happens at the end.

Dirk Sox lies dead with a bullet in his heart on the floor of the Last Hope Saloon in Splodge City, Wyoming. A pistol smokes in a shaking hand.

Now go back six months and show Dirk arriving in Splodge City. The reader is now hooked on finding out which of the characters Dirk meets in Splodge will be the one to gun him down. Will it be Teeny-bitty Kitty, short-of-stature barmaid and secret Dirk admirer? Or was it Judge Snudge who bears a grudge? Or Fife, the

15-year-old fighter? Or Unwin Loser, Kitty's unrequited love? The only way to find out is to read the book.

You have all your hooks and clues in place, and you have plotted your hero's way to a brilliant climax. But you have still got to avoid the 'one leap and she was free' pitfall. Loose ends must be tied up, good must prevail and evil be punished, but not all in the final paragraph. The end of your book needs to be planned as carefully as the beginning.

In a particularly gruelling or draining book, it might be as well to add a comic or soothing codicil to the final chapter. That is not to say that all books need a happy ending, but most publishers and book purchasers do like readers to experience a 'feel-good factor' in some shape or form between a book's covers.

High drama or fraught emotion can benefit greatly from moments of calm or comedy. Shakespeare knew this, often throwing 'crowd pleasing' comic sketches in among all the blood-letting and mayhem. Such scenes not only relieve the tension, but help to throw the more serious elements into sharp relief. Several successful television series and feature films have adopted the comedy-drama format, and many heroes are now heard to wisecrack relentlessly in even the uttermost extremity. 'Issue' fiction can deal with traumatic and upsetting real-life situations. Whilst conveying a 'you are not alone' message, or depicting another's experience, do we really want children reading relentlessly depressing material without a glimmer of hope or humour? Even tragedy can contain elements of farce.

This leads us to another topic of particular relevance to children's writing. It is usually preferable for a hero to outwit or outsmart a villain than to clobber the villain over the head with a large rock. Children like plenty of action; they want the plot to take off like an express train and hurtle breathlessly to its climax, but it is part of your job as a *responsible* author to make sure that any violence is put firmly in context. The more down-to-earth the setting of your story, the more important it is to show violence as a painful aberration and one to be avoided at all costs.

If your story is reliant on some level of violence, then bear in mind that there is a big difference between 'cartoon' violence and real-life violence. Be sure to show the consequences of violent acts, not just in terms of immediate pain, but in a wider context of long-term psychological and physiological damage. Whether your work is aimed at the middle fiction or young adult audience, check other books of a similar nature to determine your parameters for potentially controversial areas such as violence, swearing and sex.

Revising

You will be very fortunate if the first version of a your story turns out to be perfect. The only 'perfect' idea is the one that sits inside your head. Once you start trying to tease it out into the real word, it will get battered and bent and knocked about endlessly.

> *The hardest thing I learnt was not to be lazy. Write and rewrite, leave it to mature and rewrite. If 'it's good enough, it'll do' it's not good enough, it won't do.*

Often, published authors later spot sections in their books that could have been improved. An author commissioned to produce a book will be given a deadline by which that book must be handed over. That deadline dictates the point where revising has to stop.

How do you create your own revision cut-off point (or date) when there is no one around to wrest the manuscript out of your grasp? There is no simple answer to this one. Some authors will simply mark a date in their diary and keep to that.

> *Writing is work. Set a deadline if one hasn't been set for you and live like a hermit!*
>
> *It helps to arrange a date to show it to a friend.*

As with many aspects of the art and skill of writing, you have to develop a feel for 'balance'. On the one hand, you do not want to present a publisher with something that looks half-finished. But on the other hand, editors have a role to play and a particular editor may well have an entirely different view on how your book should be tidied up.

You could easily spend months and months fine-tuning your book until it is a lovely thing to behold, but how are you going to feel when a publisher says, 'We quite like it, but it needs polishing'?

The response is to revise and revise until the book says what you wanted it to say, and says it in as grammatically accurate a way as you can manage. Very, very few books ever enter the bookshops without editorial fingerprints on them. One author said:

> *I can spend months or even years 'living' with a book before finally getting around to writing it. By this time I have stacks of notes, including lengthy conversations. I plot the book chapter by chapter, very carefully, and attach each 'note' to the relevant chapter. I then do my first draft by hand. I then type a draft, make corrections, type a good copy, make more corrections, photocopy the final version, and make yet more corrections when my editor comes back with comments.*

If your book tells a good story in a professional manner and thus grabs the attention of a publisher, you will be given plenty of opportunity to revise it later.

Editors will generally have a 'hands-on' approach to your book once it has been accepted. It is not unusual for an author to be told their book will be accepted on provision that the author is prepared to rewrite large portions. What this means is that the editor has seen that certain appealing 'something' in the book, but feels you have not exploited that 'something' properly. At this point you are entitled to decline the editor's suggestions, but a more *professional* approach is to give very careful consideration to what you are being told. After all, as a new author you must be prepared to listen and bow to professional advice if you want to get published.

> *Editor*: I've read your book, and there's a lot in it that I like. Would you be prepared to completely rewrite it for us?
>
> *Author*: Yes.
>
> *(Six months later)*
>
> *Editor*: Well, I've had a chance to read your revised manuscript and I think it's much improved. Now, would you like to go away and rewrite the final two-thirds of it?
>
> *Author* (*teeth gritted*): Yes.
>
> *(Six months later)*

Editor: You're almost there. I've made six pages of comments about the areas I think you need to reconsider, but on the whole I really like it.

(Six months later)

Editor: Well done. We'll take it. There, that wasn't so difficult, was it?

Revision methods

How you go about revising your work will depend heavily on how you approach your work in the first place.

If you are working in long-hand, then hopefully you will have taken our advice and left every other line blank and incorporated wide margins. This will allow you a reasonable amount of space for alterations. If you find you need to insert entire scenes, say, in the middle of page 11, then write the scene on separate sheets and number them 11a, 11b and so on, as well as making yourself very clear, highlighted notes on the original manuscript to remind yourself of where the scenes are to be inserted. Never ever assume you will remember these things. Always leave yourself coherent notes. For all you know, you may not have the chance to go over this work again for months, and by then may have forgotten those great extra ideas.

A computer makes the task of revision much easier. Even a relatively inexpensive system will allow you to do all the editing you could wish before a hard copy (printed paper copy) is produced. A computer will even allow you to shift entire sections of the book around at will and effortlessly insert, delete and correct your book to your heart's content.

You may be two-thirds through revising a book when a new idea occurs to you. The only problem being that it will require some judicious back-tracking through parts of the book already written in order to seed properly. If you are on a creative crest you may not want to go back over these points straight away. Jot down the change you have come up with and give it some thought; you can easily set to with more revisions at a later date.

At the risk of sounding obvious, do try to be consistent. If you have stated in Chapter 13 that the electricity has been cut off in the house, it does you no credit if a character blithely switches a light on in Chapter 14. If you decide to have a discarded inhaler as a clue, make sure that the person who discarded it has been shown to be an asthmatic earlier in the book. Some authors will make up a card index or filing system for each character and scene. Details will include physical aspects of characters – brown eyes, black hair and so on – and sketches perhaps of the layout of significant buildings along with descriptions. Children have a great eye for minor detail, and will quickly spot any mistakes.

Always reread your work with an alert mind. Check for inaccuracies youself. Was so-and-so at work on the day of the arson attack, or were they off sick? Does everything make sense? Does it all flow? Might it work better if the scene between Kevin and Dolores took place after the scene where Peter is discovered lurking under the bed in Mr Ponsonby's house?

Sometimes you may find that the simple effort of shifting scenes around will work wonders. Be brave, and be prepared to jettison much-loved scenes if it turns out that they are irrelevant to the main thrust of the story. Nothing need ever be wasted, and a scene which does not work in one story, might well work successfully in another.

Hitting publishers' preferred word-targets takes experience, so the chances are that you will need to add to or take away from your story before it will approach the approved length, (not that you should feel that you are chained to a specific length if your book has other ideas). Let the story wind itself out naturally and leave concerns over precise word-lengths to the publisher. A good book will not be rejected because it is a few thousand words over or under a publisher's preferred target.

Say you have the whole plot in your head: no glaring contradictions, no gaps, no problems. It all flows seamlessly. Or does it? One of the problems for an author is that you can sometimes be too close to your book to spot omissions which, to a fresh eye, are horribly obvious.

This is where joining an authors' group will come in handy, or you could show your manuscript to a trusted friend. An objective eye may see things that you have entirely overlooked. The old saying, 'can't see the wood for the trees' is especially pertinent here.

Putting the script away, rather than rushing to the postbox immediately can also help. Forget about it for a few days (or longer), and then read it with a fresh and objective eye. You may know exactly what happens in your book; after all, you have got the whole thing nicely sorted out in your mind. Unless you write everything down clearly, you may find a reader unable to take that 'obvious' step from A to C, for the simple reason that you never actually explained B! Once an agent asked an author, 'How did the diamond ring get in the river?', to which the author replied, 'The swan in the High Street swallowed it!' 'Aha,' said the agent, 'but you haven't told the reader that!'

Exercise 13

Pick a topic, any topic – a recent day out, a description of your home, a birthday party. Anything you like. Now, with the aid of a watch, egg-timer or whatever, write on this subject for five minutes. Do not cross anything out. Try not to pause for thought. Imagine this as a kind of 'stream of consciousness' exercise. Put pen to paper (or whatever) and just go for it!

Put this work away until the following day, or at very least, much later the same day. Take it out again and reread what you have written. Spend ten minutes revising it. Note the ways in which the original has been improved. Is it longer or shorter? In either event, examine what you have done and think about why it is better.

Writer's block

What is writer's block? It is that day when you sit yourself down for a quiet stint of creativity and then find yourself, several hours later, still staring blankly at a blank sheet of paper or a blank computer screen.

Writer's block can be caused by a lot of different factors. Often it results from outside stress. If your life is in some major turmoil, the chances are that you are not going to be able to concentrate on your writing.

The first question to ask yourself is whether these external stresses can be removed? If the gas company has decided to spend a couple of weeks digging up the road outside your writing-place, can you set yourself up somewhere else until they have finished?

Might the problem be alleviated if you altered your writing routine? Are you trying to write too often? Theoretically you might be able to write for 15 hours at a stretch, but if the creative part of your brain works only for two hours before needing a rest to recharge, then the other 13 hours will be a waste of your time, and desperately frustrating to boot! Two authors suggested the following:

> *I start every morning by describing the view from my window. It looks different every day. That helps my brain to start working creatively and the routine puts me in the right frame of mind to go on to other writing. I find this particularly helpful if I have got stuck. It seems to free my mind, even if only enough to make some notes – at least I have done something.*

> *I must write something during my office hours, even if it's a sentence of rubbish which I'll delete tomorrow, but the fact of struggling with it, and finding what I don't want, is enough to make the next day's stint much easier.*

You could be stuck in mid-plot with no idea of where to go next. Do not worry, you are in good company. By his own admission, whilst writing *The Lord of the Rings*, J. R. R. Tolkien was stuck in the caverns of Moria for an entire year before coming up with a way forward for his characters. Write one line if that is all you can manage, or put the work you are stuck on away and write something entirely different. A letter to a friend or a newspaper might be all you need to unlock your creativity.

Have a root through your Ideas File. Perhaps a way forward lies hidden in there somewhere. Discuss the plot with a friend or with a group of children: as we said before, a fresh eye can work wonders, and a fresh mind may come up with a solution that might never have occurred to you. Brainstorming sessions can throw up all manner of intriguing ideas.

One word of advice. When brainstorming with someone, do not instantly dismiss their ideas, no matter how feeble you may consider them privately. Friends may very quickly clam up if they get the feeling that you think they are talking rubbish and, you never know, their forty-third idea may be just the one you've been searching for!

Another approach could be to open a dictionary or newspaper at random until an inspirational word or thought emerges. This may sound a little strange, but we have been told it really does work.

On the other hand, you may find that putting the work aside for a few days will do the trick. Have a change of scene, do something new, go for a long walk. Redundant as this advice may sound, the best bet is to stop worrying.

As one editor put it to us, 'We're not exactly dealing with brain surgery here. It's not that important!'

6 | WORKING WITH ILLUSTRATIONS

Overview

In this chapter we will be dealing with the craft of linking words and pictures together to make a coherent, convincing and entertaining whole. In general, the younger the reader appeal, the less words there will be to each picture.

Some books, especially those aimed at the middle fiction age range (8–12 year-olds), may have occasional illustrations, say, at the beginning or the end of chapters, or a few pictures scattered throughout the text, just to enliven the appearance of the book.

In graphic novels, the entire story is set out in comic-strip form. Adults are also interested in this type of presentation and there are many graphic novels aimed directly at this market.

Any books linking words and pictures requires the author to have some contact with an illustrator. The very least contact you may have would be in a book brightened by occasional line drawings. At the other end of the scale, you may find yourself working from scratch with an illustrator on a joint-effort picture book, where the words and pictures grow up together as your story evolves.

Illustrated books

To go back to the beginning, books for the very youngest start with plastic bath-time books, board books or cloth books. These are deliberately chewable, soakable, scrunch-up-able and carefully manufactured to endure the worst a small child can inflict on them. At their simplest, these books may have pictures and no text at all, bound together to be looked at and sucked as the mood takes. A basic alphabet book could come next, with each letter illustrated by a big, bright picture: 'A for Apple', 'B for Boat', 'C for Cat', and so on.

Following on from simple alphabet books, as mentioned previously, are those books where the pictures would be accompanied by a single word: 'House', 'Cat', 'Boat', 'Dog', 'Tree', 'Flower', 'Car', 'Cow' – an eight-page book already.

Writing and having one of these books published is nowhere near as simple as it may seem. For a start, these books will mostly be made up 'in house'; the ideas will be developed almost entirely by people within the publishing house, or concocted solely by the illustrator – after all, it does not take a literary genius to come up with a full-page picture of a cat that could well be accompanied by the word 'Cat'. For slightly older readers, the wording might be 'The cat sat on the mat in a hat' – and so on up the age range: 'Puzzledust the wizard's cat wore a pointed hat when she helped her master weave his wonderful spells.' These different texts could all be used to accompany exactly the same picture.

Unless you can come up with something very original, you are going to experience difficulty in finding a publisher for this sort of book. Most ideas in this line have already been thought of, worked out and published. Sorry to be repetitive, but you really need to research the marketplace very thoroughly before expending a lot of effort on these types of book.

Once children pass the 'chew-it-and-see' stage at, say, 3 years old, we enter the realms of what is known as the '32-page picture book'. These picture books contain a simple story in 32 pages which the child will be able to follow with a parent, guardian, teacher or relative, from an older sister or brother to a grandparent. Despite their seeming simplicity, these 500-or-so-word books are very difficult to write because there is no margin for error. They usually involve a full-page coloured picture accompanied by a small block of large-print text.

Illustration fashions and tastes change over time. You need only to look at some older picture books to realize this fact; pictures that may have been all the rage 20 years ago may nowadays seem quite old-fashioned and out of date. Similarly, the type of story which may have interested publishers a decade ago may no longer be of interest today. Time moves on inexorably, and no publisher wants to be thought of as being behind the times. Different countries also have widely differing tastes for illustration styles.

Printing and binding

If you are particularly interested in writing for picture books, you may well find it useful to read a specialist book detailing the printing process. (Such technical background falls outside the remit of this book, and we recommend you research for yourself on how a book is actually made.) With such a specialist title you will learn a good deal about printing processes and thereby gain better understanding of picture books. Very briefly, picture books are constructed in 'signatures' or multiples of eight (hence the name 32-page picture books: 32 being 8 × 4). Thus, eight pages are printed at one time on one large sheet of paper which is folded, trimmed, and bound into book form. As you look at the spine of a hardback book, you will see how these signatures are bound together by being sewn into multiples and then fitted together between thick card covers. (Your research will prove that all books are printed and bound using this multiple-of-eight method, into 32, 48 or 64 pages and so on.)

By their nature, hardbacks are more costly than paperbacks. However, in the picture book market, the fact that hardbacks last a lot longer than paperbacks do in young hands means that publishers will produce picture books as hardbacks. The sewing together of the signatures also increases the strength and durability of a hardback. The more a paperback picture book is used and loved, the sooner it will fall apart, whilst a hardback will endure.

On the whole, picture books are larger than books intended for older readers. This takes into account the importance of the size of illustrations. A small child will probably spend much longer looking at the pictures than they will listening to the text being read, and the larger the format of the book, the easier it is for the child to pick out and point to things in the illustrations which are of interest.

Bookshops often display picture books face-out as a purchasing enticement; after all, a book of thirty-two pages does not have much of a spine to attract the casual browser. From the point of view of the author of such a book, this is very good news indeed. A face-out picture book could easily fill as much visual space in a store as a dozen, spine-out, regular-sized books, and makes for excellent publicity.

Books intended for beginner readers (that is, those children who are able to read simple things for themselves) will tend to be longer than picture books, but still in the multiple-of-eight format (48, 64, 96 pages) until it heads into middle fiction territory (8–12-year-olds) of 144, 160, 176 pages and upwards.

Whilst we are on the subject of printing, you may have noticed that in some books there are what seem to be 'left over' blank pages at the end (you should now be in a position to understand how this happens). This is caused by the text of the book not fitting perfectly into the multiple-of-eight format. Usually only a couple of blank pages are left at the back of a book, as the publishers do their best to juggle the page breaks and typefaces to avoid too many blanks.

A modern paperback book is bound in a quite different way to hardback books. The printed and folded sheets are ground flat at the spine and glued into the covers. These days there is less chance of you breaking the spine of a paperback and watching all the pages flutter to the ground like confetti. The glue now used to hold paperbacks together is intended to keep the book in one piece for over 20 years – and glue technology is improving all the time. Even if dropped in the bath, a paperback should not come unstuck.

Publishers' time

A common question authors ask is why their picture book is taking so long to be printed and published. This is a very understandable query. Publishers tend to plan entire years ahead. For example, an editor might call you in the New Year to say that your book will be published in January. But the editor is not talking about *this* January; they are projecting into next year. This is called 'publishers' time' and is something you will need to get used to. A 12-month wait between acceptance of a book and its publication is quite normal, and 18 months to two years quite usual.

Why? It is certainly not because the book is sitting around being ignored for months on end. A lot of editorial and production processes have to be completed, and various elements co-ordinated. The jacket of a hardback book may be printed by a totally different company from the one which is printing and folding the pages. These items need then to be brought together for binding either at the printers or by a separate binder. Add to that the fact that these companies may well be in entirely different countries, and you will begin to appreciate how the time passes.

Until now we have been concentrating on simple picture books, but a quick browse in a bookshop will quickly throw up other varieties. Pop-up books are also published, where the process of opening the page pulls up cut-out sections to create a three-dimensional effect. Lift-the-flap books also proliferate, as do books where the child pulls a tag or turns a fitted card wheel to reveal hidden aspects of a picture. Similarly, cut-out books sell well, as do 'paper engineering' books in which older readers are shown how to make trains or houses or whatever out of prepressed-out and coloured shapes.

Again, think hard and take a good look around the market before you embark on such a project. Although successful 'activity' books sell well, they are very expensive to produce and a publisher will need to be convinced that a large audience exists before they will take on a book of this type. At the time of writing this book, we were able to find only a couple of companies in the whole of the UK who were prepared to print a lift-the-flap book, and even they observed that a cheaper quote could be found in countries where the manual labour which such books need is cheaper.

Colour printing and co-editions

Colour printing is a very expensive process and consequently publishers will be wary of what they are prepared to produce. Indeed, publishers will often take samples of text and some illustration layouts or spreads to foreign countries and book fairs in the hope of bringing out a co-edition (that is, a joint production) funded between two companies in order to keep costs down

It is important to understand the significance of these co-editions. It is all to do with keeping 'unit costs' low. The more books a publisher can print in one run, the cheaper each book will be to produce (the unit cost). It is exactly the same process whereby supermarkets are usually able to sell items more cheaply than a corner shop. They buy in bulk at a discounted price, and the saving can be passed on to the consumer.

In exactly the same way, if a publisher can be assured of good international sales of an expensive-to-produce book, then they will be prepared to print a large number and thereby keep their costs down. Co-editions guarantee a market in at least one other country, and could mean doubling the initial print-run of a book. If a publisher, of any book, can find a foreign publisher to come in with them, then translations can be made, and the books for both countries can be printed together by the same printer. The finished copies can then be sold and shipped to the publisher ready to go straight into the shops in that country.

Full-colour printing (also known as 'four-colour printing', because virtually all colours can be derived from a combination of four basic colours) is expensive, especially on the sort of good quality, glossy paper that does justice to the illustrations. Hence, a publisher will need to be totally convinced that your picture book idea is financially viable before going ahead with the project.

The bottom line for the beginner is: forget ABC-type books, whether they are in verse, or rhyming couplets or any sort of poetry, or whether they are simple 'K is for kangaroo' books. Publishers are unlikely to take on such a book unless the author has a proven track record or has created something stunningly inventive.

Text for picture books

If you are still undaunted by the difficulties of breaking into the picture book market, let alone the constraints of writing very short stories, then you will need to know what sort of text lengths are required. A 32-page picture book can have as little as fourteen words or as many as 1,000, depending upon the age group targeted.

Here is an example of a 32-page spread. This gives you 12 double-page spreads in which to tell your story, once you have discounted the end-papers, the page with publisher's information on it and the title page. So, as you can see, in a 32-page picture book, your story probably will not begin until page 6, and might have to be wrapped up by page 29 if there is a repeated end-paper. Your narrative will have to be spaced fairly evenly through these 12 spreads. You should not have a big chunk of prose on one spread followed by only a couple of words on the next (and yes, there are always

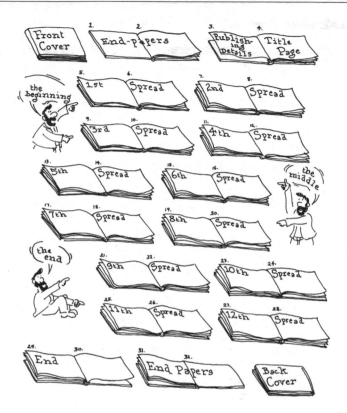

exceptions!). The story needs to balance out, and this can be very difficult.

Your text can appear on these spreads either in a block in some 'empty' space (space deliberately left by the illustrator) or along the top of the spread, or along the bottom. It can even appear in two blocks, one on each page of the spread, or entirely on one page with the weight of the illustration dominating the other. (Check out the design layouts of popular, and/or award-winning picture books.) It is easier for children who are learning to read, or those with sight or learning difficulties, to read typeface printed on a white surface, rather than type which is overlaid on a coloured background.

All these things will need to be taken into consideration when constructing your story.

Think visually

It is essential, too, to think *pictures*. Anything that can be seen by the child need not be mentioned in the prose. You do not need to describe characters, scenery or action which is going to appear in picture form. Your words are like a rope tying a series of brightly coloured balloons together. Pictures, by their nature and notwithstanding the amount of action depicted, are static. They can only capture the instant. Your task as the author is to link those static moments together into a coherent narrative. Never waste words describing things: use the few words you are allowed to push the story on and to explain to the reader how they get from picture A to picture B and so on. A successful author thinks visually.

Naturally, you will have very definite ideas about what your characters look like or how their surroundings should be depicted. These details can be conveyed separately. Write down all such information and present it with the manuscript. You may also have thoughts on the layout and type of pictures you would like, but be prepared for a publisher to have their own ideas and a 'house style' to follow.

Then again you may have no thoughts at all of how the illustrations will mesh with the text. This is not a problem: an illustrator's job is to visualize your words. But you still need to keep your eyes on the beginning–middle–end balancing act.

On the whole, the middle of your story should take up as much space as the beginning and the end put together, if not slightly more. In a 32-page book, this would mean the beginning should take two or three spreads, the middle would take six to eight spreads, and the end another two to three. These are only guide-lines, but it does serve to give you an idea of the sort of balance for which you should aim. Another thing to avoid is the gabbled ending, where the story suddenly reads like it has had rockets attached – all because the author has not left enough room to bring the story to a well-rounded conclusion!

Balance has to be achieved through the pacing of the text as well as the pacing of the story being told. In a 500-word, 12-spread book, you should try to accompany each spread with about 40 words.

Picture-book stories need plenty of movement. There is no room for long static conversations between characters. Just as we wrote in Chapter 5 about the importance of ending chapters with cliff-hangers, in a picture book every spread has to be a cliff-hanger in its own right.

The really successful picture books are those which manage to include a kind of 'subtext' which will engage the attention of the adult reader as well as the basic story which absorbs the child. Take a look at a book such as *Owl Babies* by Martin Waddell (the subtext story is a child's natural fear of being left by its mother) and the Ahlbergs' books (where many 'jokes' are told in the detailed background illustrations). If an adult is going to be forced to read a much-loved picture book to an insistent child for 365 consecutive days, the successful ones will be those with glorious illustrations, or storylines which never cease to appeal to their audience.

Varying the scenery

The view needs to vary, meaning that your story cannot really be set wholly in one character's bedroom, unless some pretty extraordinary *visual* things happen in there, or the bedroom can be viewed from several different angles in an imaginative way. The scene must be visually stimulating on every page. The best way of learning how to do this is to read published picture books. Observe how text and illustration blend together in these books. Or try a different approach: block out the text with your hand or a sheet of paper, and see how much of the plot you can follow simply by looking at the pictures.

In a well-plotted picture book, the pictures should almost tell the story on their own.

The same kind of effect can be achieved by turning the sound down on a television whilst watching cartoons. See how much of the story is carried by the pictures. Your text need only convey about 50 per cent of the story; let the illustrations do the rest. That is what they are there for.

Example

Text: Mum was late!

Picture: Harassed-looking mum with gaping handbag, open coat and hair all over the place is pulling child out of house. The child is fully dressed, but Mum is still in her nightie and slippers. By the expression on the child's face, Mum clearly does not usually take him out in her night-clothes.

The effect of this on the reader is to whet their appetite for what is to come next. Why is Mum late? Why does she have a nightie on out of doors? What happens when she realizes how she is dressed? Will the little boy tell her that she has forgotten to get dressed, or leave her to realize on her own? Where are they going?

All conveyed by three words and an intriguing illustration.

Or the same picture could be accompanied by something quite different:

'Kevin had the feeling that this wasn't going to be just another ordinary day.'

This is a significantly more complex text, intended for an older reader.

You need to establish a context and some interesting characters as soon as possible. If the story is to be told through the eyes of a single character, then that character must be shown from page one.

In a ghost story, the first picture may be of Harriet in her haunted bedroom. This establishes her as the heroine. On the other hand, the ghost may be the hero, and Harriet merely an interloper. Such a story could begin with the ghost peacefully lying on the bed and reading, and continue with the ghost being rudely disturbed by Harriet charging in wearing hobnailed boots, swinging a football rattle over her head and shouting loudly. The reader would instantly sympathize with the ghost and would appreciate that the story was to be told from the disturbed ghost's point of view.

A mouse, living in the skirting-board, has its life made a misery by the endless conflict between a well-established ghost and a young ghost-hunter. The story would then revolve around the mouse's attempts to get rid of both the ghost and the ghost-hunter – or possibly to come up with some way of convincing them into peaceful cohabitation.

Exercise 14

Write a text for a 12-spread story in as few words as possible. Your challenge for this exercise is to have the story begin in one place and end in that same place: it could be a garden, kitchen, beside the dinosaur display in a museum, or wherever. The other spreads must each contain a different scene for visual stimulation. Your aim is for a coherent story, which moves along, as well as keeping to that good old beginning–middle–end structure.

No, it is not easy, but if it is any consolation, a successful picture book text could earn an advance as large as that of a 40,000-word novel!

Things to remember

Voice of the narrator

When writing for the youngest age groups, it is best to keep the voice of the narrator well out of the picture. An example to avoid is having text which says 'Can you guess what happens next?' or 'Can you see where Squishy the Moose is hiding?' Small children find this kind of text very difficult to comprehend, especially those still learning to read.

Tense

Similarly, avoid complicated use of tenses. Keep the story in a single tense and keep the sentences short and to the point. In picture books especially, adjectives and adverbs should not be necessary – the illustrations will deal with all such flourishes. If a heroine is wearing her favourite red scarf, the only comment needed in the text is that it is a favourite, and not that it is red. If a hero is entering a building with a sign outside saying 'Swimming Pool', then there is no need to write: 'Zac was going to the swimming baths for a swim.'

Internationality

In remembering the importance of the international market for the viability of these books, it is worth knowing that publishers may be reluctant to take on a book which is understandable only in its country of origin. A book published in the UK may not be acceptable to other countries if it is filled with things such as people delivering milk to the house, police officers with their traditional domed helmets or animals such as hedgehogs. Such details are not universally understood.

Likewise, in the UK the post is generally delivered through a front-door letterbox by a postman/woman, but in the USA the mail is more usually left in an external mailbox by the mailman/woman. This is a small point, but to say to an American that the post has arrived will conjure up visions of a length of wood being delivered rather than letters. Similarly, acceptable phrases, words, jokes, homilies and superstitions in one country, may be meaningless or even misunderstood by another. A black cat which crosses your path in the UK is considered a lucky omen. In Italy it is seen as a very unlucky omen! (In the UK, adult books are those of any subject aimed at adult readers, in the USA, the words 'adult books' refer to those of an erotic nature!) Michael Coleman's picture book, *The Mum Who Was Made of Money*, is a universally understood parental problem, and the book has sold into many countries. *The Very Hungry Caterpillar* by Eric Carle, and *The Snowman* by Raymond Briggs are known worldwide, but an ABC or a rhyming text may not translate at all.

Such prejudices work in both directions, and a UK publisher may well not purchase a foreign picture book which deals with things that make little sense outside the country where it was written. The thing to keep in mind when writing your story is that it should not be too parochial. A child on the other side of the world should be able to grasp the significance of what is going on as well as a child who lives two streets away from you.

Fashion trends

Fashions and trends of acceptability change, and you would do well to take time out to research what is not acceptable in a picture book. Violence, sex, gore and general mayhem are obvious taboos, but these days there is also a reluctance to publish books where the boys go out doing adventurous things whilst the girls stay at home with their mother preparing lunch for them in between washing dolly's clothes and vacuuming the house.

Other stories to avoid are those about dragons. Trust us, dragons have been done to death! Similarly, Betty the Bunny and Bodge the Badger who live in candy-coloured cottages in Bunger Town should be avoided, as should most anthropomorphic stories. (In some countries, stories about pigs, goats or cows doing crazy or anthropomorphic actions go down really well, yet in other cultures, where these animals are considered either sacred or taboo, such stories would never find a publisher.) Of course, one day, when you are a rich and famous children's author you may write a unique dragon and bunny story, and get away with it!

Setting the text

Presenting your picture book to the publisher

To remind you, a picture book is not the same as a story book. A picture book has narrative illustrations; a story book has an illustrated text and is intended for older readers. Can you see the difference? A story book story could be read without the illustrations, whereas a picture book story would lose a lot from the absence of the pictures.

Let us concentrate on picture books. As far as illustrations are concerned, unless you are a very talented professional with experience of illustrating children's books, the best advice we can give you is to *leave illustrations well alone*. There are various ways to present the text of a picture book story. Some authors merely type out: 'Page 1', followed by the line(s) of text, and then use a fresh sheet of paper for page 2. Others will present as follows:

Page 1

Mum was late!

(Illustration of harassed-looking mum ... and so on)

By all means include a pictorial (stick-people) reference or a separate layout to help explain some complex visual requirement. You can even suggest perspectives and other potential ideas. However, the editor, art director, design department and/or publisher may have other ideas.

Often, when an editor reads a submission, they may be looking for a story to suit artists they already have in mind to use. In this case, a particular visual style will already be established into which your story might fit. At other times, an editor will seek an appropriate illustrator and may consult you for your opinion as to the final choice. It is fairly unlikely that you would enter an editor's office with your picture book idea fully formed and be allowed to say, 'I want it exactly like this, thanks'.

Many illustrators and artists have their own agents with a wealth of talent on their books for an editor to view. As in all things, publishers will generally prefer to use an illustrator whose work has proved popular, rather than use an unknown. Back to that old catch-22 situation.

One prospect more disturbing than having your picture book illustrations discarded is if you have asked a friend to illustrate your book only to have your story accepted and their amateurish hard work rejected. You will then be in the awkward position of having to suppress your own euphoria while you break it to your friend that their labours were in vain.

Even an excellent draughtsman with a lot of talent may well fall into some of the more obvious traps when they try to illustrate a book. Have you considered that a face drawn across a double-page spread will look decidedly odd when the nose vanishes into the cleft between the pages. There are other important techniques and limitations, ranging from colour processes to text overlays which an illustrator should know about when working on picture books. Leave the artwork to the professionals, unless you are one of a rare and fortunate breed of author–illustrators. In general, do not take advantage of friends whom *you* think can draw, nor submit your own work unless you really know the business of illustrating children's books.

Story books

Whereas picture books spread the workload equally between words and pictures, story books have more than twice the text, are usually smaller in size, and rely much less heavily on the artist's input. An average story book text-length starts at around 2,500 words. The story will be split into several chapters and spaced out with plenty of illustrations.

As with picture books, the story should be well balanced and full of interest and movement, but the balancing act between words and pictures need not be quite so precise. The 2,500 plus word length allows much more room for dialogue and for brief descriptions of things which the illustrator will be depicting.

Some story books are illustrated in colour throughout; some are part-colour, part-black-and-white line illustration; and others are black-and-white line only. Check 'beginner reader's' series for styles. A brief trawl through your library will show you the range of illustrations used in story books, from the meticulously detailed and highly realistic full-colour works to the kind of cartoons that are so fluent that they look really easy – until you try it!

Let us say you have submitted a beginner reader story book text. The editor is interested but wants you to make alterations before acceptance. These alterations may be intended to clarify or brighten the plot, or to spread the action out a little (especially if your story takes a little while to get off the ground and then ends all in a rush on the last page). Or the editor may think you have included some piece of grammar which is too complex for the intended readership, or a word or two which need to be exchanged with something more simple.

By now you will understand the style and the sort of words you must fit into the scope of the target readership, but an editor may still make suggested alterations which change your original phrase 'inharmonious discord' to 'terrible noise' without losing its sense.

Once a text has been accepted, the publisher will work on marrying your story to an artist. As we have said, generally the publisher will choose the illustrator and an in-house design team will work on the layout. You may well not have much of an input at this stage, save to be informed of which artist the publisher has chosen and being sent examples of their work.

Next you will be sent proofs of the text set out as it will appear in the finished book, with gaps left for the illustrations. Then you should get to see some roughs (usually loosely sketched drawings) of the artwork. Sometimes the first thing you will see are colour photocopies of the finished pictures. Hopefully (but sadly not always the case), you will be asked for your input at the rough artwork stage, so that you can add your ideas, or point out any errors. We have seen picture books where one character had a moustache which appeared and disappeared, and another where a character's jumper changed colour and style throughout the book!

Detailed illustrations could take an artist weeks or months to complete, so this process will take some time.

Moving on up the age range from story books, you will discover middle fiction books with, say, 10 or so line drawings and maybe small vignettes at the beginnings or endings of chapters. As with picture and story books, you will be kept informed of what is happening with the illustrations, but on the whole, scenes to be illustrated and the placing of illustrations will be out of your hands.

As you can see, the older the reader, the less pictures their books generally have. Of course, there are exceptions to this, one of which is the graphic novel style, intended to attract an older but somewhat reluctant readership. Text for graphic novels has to follow the same style as that for photo-stories in teen-magazines. It is almost a cartoon format and written mostly in dialogue with only very brief explanations. If this area appeals, do your research, study the layouts, and write and ask publishers for any briefs they may have for their series.

Book covers

A lot of time, thought and effort goes into deciding what should appear on the cover of a book. The audience for which the book is intended is considered carefully and the cover design is aimed specifically at grabbing their attention.

Mystery, ghost and thriller books will probably be given dark covers full of shadows and eerie colours. Cheerful or comedy books will have bright covers and show bunches of smiling, happy people so that the potential reader will want to get to know these characters and enter their lives. Children's publishers are becoming more and more inventive, and are taking cover artwork very seriously to produce stunning jackets and covers which can outshine many adult-trade marketing-conscious publishers.

The look of a book cover is created from several elements. If it is part of a series, then there has to be a series title somewhere. Then the title of the individual book and the author's name, followed by an engaging, stimulating picture, photograph, or montage intended to send the books leaping down from the shelves and into children's hands.

If you have specific ideas for the cover of your book, an editor or publisher will be glad to hear from you about it, but keep in mind that behind the editor are design and marketing teams who probably know a lot more about the intended market than you do. Once again, your opinion will be sought and hopefully you will be kept informed at every step but, to be honest, as one editor told us in a moment of weakness, if you were to express disapproval of a cover at a late stage, the chances of you being able to make fundamental changes at that point are limited, not least because the artist will already be under commission and money will have been spent.

Nevertheless, as an author to whom we spoke testified, it is possible to effect changes. He was shown a 'finished' cover painting for one of his books only to spot that the cat in the picture was an entirely different colour from the one described in the book. The next time he saw the picture, the cat had been repainted.

The thing to remember is that you are probably an author, not an illustrator. You may wish to express your views on how a work of yours should be illustrated, but there are going to be plenty of people around with much more experience and expertise who are worth listening to.

Illustrated non-fiction

Most of the same rules apply to illustrated non-fiction as they do for illustrated fiction. However, non-fiction books are far more design led than fiction, as the text and illustrations are integrated across the pages. It is terribly important that you, as the author, see the rough artwork before it is approved for completion. Presumably you will have researched your subject and be knowledgeable about what is correct. If your topic is the internal combustion engine, then obviously any drawn illustrations (as opposed to photographs) have to be absolutely technically correct.

Photographs, too, must to be of the right subject and angle. A nonfiction work will probably have a great deal more editorial input and author guidance than a work of fiction. You may also have much more control over the suggested kind of illustrations and/or photographs to be used, unless you are writing for a series which already has a clearly defined style.

7 | MARKETS FOR FICTION

People who write

People who write for a living, or for part of their living, fall into four main categories. In our experience, they are broadly defined as:

- *Ink junkies*: the obsessives, who write because they cannot help it; putting words onto paper is the way they best interact with the outside world. They can be prolific letter writers and can also be found on committees as they are excellent organizers.

- *Light-bulb people*: these are people with *ideas*; they want to get these ideas out into the world and the only obvious way of doing that is by writing them down. Sometimes this character type will flit from good idea to good idea without ever actually researching, or completing anything.

- *Drifters*: these are people who already have contact on some level with the publishing world or with the media and who slip into writing for children because it seems like a good career move. These types are often in for a rude awakening.

- *I can do that*: these are people who think that writing for children is easy, and that they can do better than the material they have seen on sale. They also think there is a crock of gold at the end of their writing rainbow.

(An author from the ink junkies category told us that he was at a launch party once where he asked one of the other authors there how she got into writing for children. She said she had worked for a publisher and, upon starting a family, went into children's writing because she could do it from home and because it was 'family friendly'.)

The point is that the work you have produced, or intend to produce, will probably be driven to some extent by the fact that you fit into one of the listed categories. All of these category types have an equal chance of success as long as they take off their rose-tinted spectacles and co-ordinate their efforts professionally.

Assessing yourself

As this chapter covers how you are going to try and sell your work, this is the time for you to take a good look at what you have done so far.

You are halfway through this book; by now you should have set up a number of things. You should have your Ideas File up and running. You should have taken yourself out and about on plenty of research fieldtrips, both into the world of bookshops and libraries, and into the 'real' world for inspiration. You may have even visited schools and/or book fairs.

The time has come for you to assess whether there is a market out there for your work. Hopefully, that raw piece of writing, or that unformed idea which first set you reading this book, has been honed and shaped by what you have read and learnt so far.

(If you have been too busy reading this book to do any work on your ideas or writing, then put this book down *immediately* and get creative!)

Now take a good, long, hard look at your work. Does it seem to you to be close to the mark, but not quite there yet? Perhaps it just needs tidying up, shortening, lengthening or better audience-targeting. The research you have undertaken should help you to address any or all of these areas.

Perhaps you have discovered that your big idea is already sitting on the shelves in a bookshop. Do not despair. Can you tackle the same idea with an entirely fresh, new approach? One famous author said that there is nothing *new* to be written, but that the job of an author was to add their own colours to an existing canvas. (There is a nice mixed metaphor for you to consider!) A very successful playwright said that a person endlessly ploughs the same furrow but is always turning up fresh material.

Your idea may still be viable even though someone else has used it before, if you can view it with your individual eye and mind and add an unusual aspect to it.

Your research will also have given you an insight into the publishing world. Which publishers seem to you most likely to be interested in the piece of work you have produced? You will save yourself an enormous amount of wasted time, effort and postage by making your initial approaches to publishers who are at least in the market for the book you have written (or are planning on writing).

The practicalities of submitting work will be dealt with in detail in Chapter 9, so we need not discuss this here. What we will discuss are the types of publishers that exist in the world of children's books.

Types of publishers

There is a great variety of publishers on the lookout for picture books, illustrated, and longer, text-only fiction. At the top end of the market are the major trade publishers whose products are distributed far and wide in bookshops, libraries, school book clubs, supermarkets, mail-order clubs, online booksellers, overseas and so on. These are mostly large corporations with their main offices in capital cities.

These large conglomerate publishers are not the whole story. There are also many, many smaller trade publishers (who often specialize in niche markets), which include family concerns and regional publishers who concentrate on producing a small number of high-quality books. In these days of desktop publishing and freelancers, such small companies can literally be run from home and are well worth investigating. Both types of companies have points for and against, as is to be expected. The big corporations have plenty of clout in the marketplace and have the ability to ensure your work is available on shelves throughout the world. However, a smaller company may be able to give you more personal attention. With these publishers you are less likely to encounter the ponderous decision-making processes that typifies larger companies, where every commission has to go through several vetting procedures before anyone is able to spend any money.

Smaller, independent publishers are quite capable of achieving very high sales figures in a quiet, unassuming way, through diligent hard work on your behalf, and through being able to concentrate on selling a small list; not to mention gaining prize-winning attention simply because their small number of products are of such a high quality. Major publishers with their sales and distribution power could be easily shamed by some of the excellent sales figures these independents achieve.

Usually both of the above types of trade publisher will pay advances and royalties.

Packagers

Another type of publisher in the marketplace is the 'packager' or 'packager publisher'. These companies will often develop an idea on their own and then approach one of the major trade publishers with the completed product, the aim being that all the major publisher has to do is pay the packager, add the book(s) to their list and set about the distribution. Packagers might approach a 'major' with anything from a single picture book to a series of books. These are also the people who may design technically complicated products which have glossy artwork, holograms, cut-outs, and so forth. They may even present the publisher with merchandising spin-offs such as boxed sets of books which may include mugs, T-shirts, cuddly toys, bookmarks or an interactive computer game.

Such products are often seen in the bargain or remainder bookshops, toy shops, high street chain-stores as well as the more usual outlets. To get an idea of how spin-off merchandising works, wait for the next Hollywood animated feature film to come out and then observe how rapidly the stores fill with a diverse range of merchandise.

Packagers are not generally geared to accepting unsolicited projects (that is, *your* idea), but a good idea suited to a particular company's style is well worth submitting. Such well-thought-out proposals, targeted appropriately, do not waste anyone's time and, even if your idea is not picked up this time, the company may well add your name to their author files and come back to you when they need someone for a particular project suited to your talents.

Packagers generally only pay originators or contributors a flat fee or one-off payment. We will go into this later, but here point out that your flat fee may look a little sick if the product you helped develop shoots off to become a major financial success.

Overseas publishers

Our shops are filled these days with cheap products of varying quality from far-flung countries. Children's books are no exception, and the material from such sources is often not of the trade publishers' mainly high standards. Author payment, if you should succeed in gaining a response and acceptance for your submission, is not usually very high. It is also difficult to monitor the accounting and sales procedures of these publishers. You have been forewarned.

Where to start

Aim for the top

When selecting publishers for your work, the best bet is to aim initially for the top: the major publishers. Ensure that the work you want to submit to them falls within the boundaries of their 'list'. (A publisher's catalogue will give you easy access to the kind of material they are producing.)

Be prepared to adapt your work to fit the requirements of an individual publisher. Your chances of getting published are increased if, as a new author, you submit work exactly suited to their needs or for an existing series. A busy editor may well choose a work that fits their needs exactly and, therefore, does not require time-consuming editorial input, over a story of equal merit which is the wrong length.

Tip-sheets

Many publishers are willing to supply 'tip-sheets' or 'briefs' which will give you an idea of their specific requirements, especially where a series is concerned. These are usually single-page outlines which detail word-count, style and content specifications. After all, if you are submitting a young adult romance, it is handy to know in advance whether kissing is allowed, whether the courting characters are permitted beyond the bedroom door, or whether they are to express their quivering devotion only by the twin-straw sharing of a strawberry milkshake in full view of sundry hawk-eyed relations.

A letter of enquiry to a publishing house accompanied by a stamped, self-addressed envelope, sent to the editor in charge of the series in which you are interested should produce a reply. You may think that a telephone call will shorten your waiting time, but this may not be the case. A busy editor may not relish the interruption of an unsolicited telephone call and you should remember that part of your task as a budding author is to keep on the good side of editors. Letters, good; phone calls, bad. And do *not* forget the self-addressed envelope: you may never hear from the publisher otherwise. One stamp may not seem to you much of a financial outlay for a company, but for a large publishing house one stamp multiplied by several hundred over the course of a year is a considerable cost for any company.

Editors do not take kindly to submissions by e-mail. Write and enquire first before you fax or e-mail. Or check the publisher's website – if they have one – for their particular requirements on the submission of work.

Longer fiction

If your first piece of work is a young adult novel, a trilogy or a sequence of linked novels, you will find that the number of publishers willing to consider your book(s) is considerably smaller. There are various reasons for this. A single book needs to be given a very high profile and a veritable mountain of publicity if it is to raise itself above all the others on the shelves and succeed. Publishers are well aware of this and are consequently interested only in work that they consider to be of a very high grade indeed. Fewer publishers have young adult fiction lists, particularly for individual titles, and these tend to be small in comparison to the mass of books for the younger age ranges. It can be argued that fewer young adults buy and read books aimed specifically at them.

Series fiction

There is a much greater call for paperback series fiction. It is much easier to sell a book of a successful series or imprint than it is to sell a one-off title.

Before you decide to write for an existing series, do make sure that more titles are being commissioned and that you have a copy of the publisher's brief. Then you should submit a proposal or synopsis and three sample chapters. For a series outline, you would also need to submit further plots, so that the publisher is able to see that the idea has prospects.

Educational fiction

There are publishers who specialize in producing fiction for the educational market. Their activities range from buying titles from trade publishers and producing their own editions mainly for schools and libraries, to creating 'in-house' reading schemes (although some publishers are now making inroads into the traditional trade outlets with an eye on potential parental purchasers).

Educational publishers also produce a wide variety of original fiction material to suit many special needs. This can range from picture books to longer fiction introducing such themes as bereavement and divorce, as well as issues for people of differing ability.

For children who find reading more of a challenge, high interest but lower reading ability books, known as 'Hi-Lo readers' are produced. These books are for children and adults who may be learning to read but who are too old to be interested in 'Percival the Parrot' picture books. Hi-Lo readers are very challenging to write, and you are advised not to attempt this without a very good idea of the areas into which you are straying.

Publishers' reading schemes will have been thoroughly researched and planned as well as having been tested in schools and focus groups. Your enquiry about writing for such schemes will probably result in the arrival of a very long and detailed outline, and sometimes even a word-list from which your text must be constructed. This is writing within very precise parameters and is not really intended for people without experience or apposite skills.

Thus, it should not be surprising to learn that educational publishers often directly approach authors and illustrators, or will commission teachers whom they know to be good writers. Such people have a good working knowledge of the way children are taught to read, the word-lists for different ages and so on. If you work in this area, you may already have the necessary expertise that educational publishers require. (A cautionary word here: sometimes even the most expert teacher may be unable to convey information well on paper; a good teacher is not necessarily going to make a good author.)

If you are interested in this area of publishing, then there may be a school or educational fair which you can attend. There you will find the appropriate publishers and you will be able to do some research before making your initial approach.

Dual-language books

Dual-language books are published for those children whose first language is not that of the country in which they are living and being educated, or for those families who are or wish to be bilingual. These books are most often seen in picture book format, in which the text appears in two languages, and are most likely to have been bestsellers in their originating language. A few publishers seek original works in this area; if you are fluent and competent in other languages, than you may find this type of work of interest.

Religion

The religious publishing market is very strong, with various publishers dedicated solely to the publication of religious or spiritual material. On the children's side, many religious publishers are on the lookout for work that fits their particular beliefs, but conveys the message in a subtle way without being didactic or 'preachy', particularly where the fiction area is concerned.

Film, television, radio and theatre

Film, television, radio and theatre is a highly specialized fiction market and very tough for a newcomer to enter. Many scriptwriters and playwrights have previous, published book-writing experience. There are specialist books and courses on screen and scriptwriting for these media which will show you how to set out a screenplay and work for film, television, radio and theatre, and you should search these out if you wish to attempt writing for these areas. The children's slice of these markets is small in comparison to the adult portion of this media cake, but expanding healthily as the number of channels increases.

Some publishers do produce fiction plays and playlets for schools and religious markets, both for trade and non-trade outlets.

Once you have gained the necessary scriptwriting skills, you should then research the television and radio listings market for details of the programme producers to whom your work could be submitted. Media listings books are also published annually, which will give you a good idea of who's who in the media world, and where to approach them. There are also media magazines and annual festivals, although we are not suggesting you travel to Cannes or elsewhere with a script under your arm. Many programmes are produced independently of the broadcasting companies and they are often seeking good ideas and new material. However, these independent companies usually have to research and then raise interest as well as finances before they can go into production. This procedure can easily take a couple of years.

Long-running series, children's soap operas and educational broadcasts frequently use different storyline writers, but you will need tenacity and luck to break into this market. (As ever we are talking about tenacity and luck coupled with thorough research and professional skill.)

The market for live theatre, ballet and dance is very small, and tends to be confined to previously published or other well-known works. Fame can follow the success of small local productions, fringe or festival successes, but short of finding a monied producer who adores your work, your best approach may be to find a theatrical agent who specializes in selling to these markets.

Payments for television and radio work generally adhere to specific guidelines for original material, adaptations, repeat fees for re-broadcasting, overseas sales and so on. These guidelines can be obtained from screenwriter societies. If you are particularly interested in this kind of work then joining one of these organizations will provide you with plenty of regular information, guidance and news of the latest market developments and legal complexities via their magazines.

Payment in all of these media areas is not the phenomenal amount that the movie-type industry hype and extravagance might lead you to believe. Few authors for these areas are given a profit percentage – however, if you wrote the book from which a big box-office success ensues, then enormous numbers of books may sell as a result.

Electronic communication

As the world of electronic communication expands and evolves, steady work can be found for computer-literate authors. This work will tend to attract flat fees as you will generally be one of a large number of authors working on a particular project. Also, the copyright of the project will belong to the producer of the electronic work or other software being developed. Work in this area could include writing sections for encyclopedias, embellishing a game based on a best-selling series of children's fiction books or writing for educational websites.

There are many conferences and shows you can attend, although some are extremely expensive. Exhibitors tend to be hardware manufacturers and software developers, displaying their abilities and wares, with very few actual publishers in attendance. Check before you go as to what exactly you can expect from a conference or show before making any expeditions.

Tracking down the original producer/creator of a software package in order to present an idea to them may be a difficult process, as they are often bought in by the publisher or especially commissioned from an independent firm. Computing and gaming magazines, shops and special supplements in educational newspapers will help you to narrow down your search.

Magazines and comics

It is unlikely that you will become rich writing for the magazine and comic market. In recent years much of the material for these markets is produced in-house, or bought in from other countries, thereby limiting your publishing chances even further. As ever, study the market and submit appropriate material for short stories, photo-stories, cartoons and so on.

Many of the comics for younger readers are based on cartoon or well-known picture book characters. The magazine publishers license the right to use these characters from the owner (licensor). Authors are then employed to adapt or write suitable material involving these characters. The licensor then usually approves the work before it can be published, and this can mean rewriting work several times until it is judged fit for publication. Material may fly back and forth, as the licensors can be very difficult to please. You will need patience!

If you are able to get into these markets, they can prove a steady source of income. Experience in these fields, the ability to work to tight schedules, and writing about characters not of your own creation can be valuable experience. Potential book publishers are impressed by an author who shows versatility. It is worthwhile developing a range of writing skills, especially if you want to make a living from being an author.

Competitions

A lot of newspapers and magazines run competitions for short stories and poetry, and some even for plays and novels. A number of competitions are annual events, so it is worth keeping you eyes and ears open. Submit material which fits the competition regulations exactly, even if that means adapting something to suit. Writing to a specific order will be a useful experience and, whilst you may not win the big prize, you may well get to see your name and possibly your work in print which could be spiritually as well as financially rewarding. Winning a competition or being published in almost any kind of format will help instil confidence in a potential publisher for your children's work, too.

Anthologies

Some publishers regularly compile seasonal or themed anthologies of short stories or poetry.

It is too difficult to second-guess what these publishers are looking for next, so find out who they are, and then ask them for information as to what is currently being commissioned. Often an independent editor or author is chosen to compile the anthology and they will have prepared a brief for their requirements. Once again, remember to write and enclose a large stamped, self-addressed envelope with all such enquiries; do not telephone!

And, finally, filler markets

There is less call for filler items in the children's market, but they include jokes and letters, as well as humorous story and information slots in appropriate magazines and newspapers. Choose those publications which will actually pay for inclusion of your material.

There are newsletters to which you can subscribe that will provide details of such work. Often they include useful information on competitions and the world of children's publishing.

8 | NON-FICTION BOOKS

Non-fiction and fiction

It would probably be just as well at this point to explain again what is meant by 'non-fiction' and 'fiction'. This has very little to do with 'truth' and a whole lot to do with 'fact'.

Everything you write has to come across to a reader as being *true*; that is, having an internal order and sense, no matter how unusual or strange that truth may be. Even the wildest cartoon or the most surreal comedy has to conform to its own inner logic, otherwise it just becomes incoherent, aimless and meaningless rambling. It is this basic created world structure that we refer to when we talk about truth.

Fact is another matter altogether. It is all to do with creating a *willing suspension of disbelief.*

It may be true that the full moon, turns respectable people into ravening werewolves, assuming that these people have previously been bitten by another werewolf. Indeed, for a werewolf story to function, this 'truth' has to be accepted, but if this truth is questioned, either the story has been very badly written or that particular reader should not be reading a werewolf yarn in the first place.

Similarly, it has to seem credible that a penniless street urchin can grow up to own a multimillion dollar international company or to become President of the USA. Such a story need not be factual and will probably benefit greatly from not being factual, but it has to 'ring true'.

Speaking of street urchins, what if you were inspired to write the history of some great plutocrat? It could be the same story: rags to riches. But if you were planning on using the actual person, and telling their life story, then you would need to ensure that you had your facts right. It is no good taking a calculated guess that so-and-so was born in a wooden shack in Kentucky and had 73 brothers and sisters who all slept in the same bed. You need to find out the facts.

A word comes floating into sight ... a familiar word ... and that word is: *research*.

Accuracy

Non-fiction calls for research on a much more rigorous level than fiction. Once you have got your basics sorted in a fictional novel, you can embroider the story with as much invented detail as you feel inclined. Not so with non-fiction. Whatever subject or area you approach, you must do it with a stringent eye on thorough research.

If you take a glance at the back of almost any biography, you will spot at once that the author seems to have used an awful lot of information from page after page of *other* books. Well, how else would you research a biography, for the sake of argument, about Napoleon? You can hardly go around asking people what he was like. They are all dead. The only sources of information are going to be books, archives and written materials.

Of course, a question to ask yourself before you stagger home, reeling from the weight of a heap of heavy historical tomes, or print out endless pages of information, is why you think the world needs another biography of Napoleon. Maybe you have come up with a fresh angle on his life and loves?

Mind you, this may not prove suitable reading for children, but you see the point: your particular new twist on the Napoleon story will require you to plough your way through scores of other factual books, gathering information, noting anomalies, linking all the background you need on which to place your own observations.

Such research will always be of fundamental importance for anything historical and, in a way, it can prove the least demanding. Realize, though, that the books that you choose for research purposes will all have their own bibliographies which demand attention. If you do not know where to draw the line, you might end up disappearing so far into the root system of the past that your own book is never finished because it becomes impossible to unravel the truth.

What if you want to write a book about the Amazon rainforests. Certainly you will be able to pick up written information, but you will also need to consider a visit to the Amazon Basin for 'field research'. If you are considering the effect of the modern world on the rainforests, then you will need to ask a few local people for their opinions. It is no good just chatting to industrialists. You are going to have to head into the jungle and speak to the indigenous people, to see what they think of things. If you are planning to write about any country or culture, you need to have experienced it from all angles for it to be an accurate and objective piece of work.

Any non-fiction book is going to take time and money: your own time and the time of people you interview or observe; and your own money, unless you are lucky enough to get a bursary or sponsorship from an interested party.

Even though you may consider yourself to be an expert in whatever field you are intending to write about, there are probably plenty of other 'experts' out there too. Though you may disagree wildly with their opinions, you will have to know what they are in order to refute them. The only way of finding out about their opinions is either to lay hands on these experts' writings, or to go and talk to the people themselves.

Faction

Previously we mentioned 'faction', and this is a good time to mention it again. Faction is dramatized fact and there is a lot of it about. It can take the form of a school play depicting important historical events:

The scene: the Atlantic Ocean in 1492

J. Tar (a sailor): Land ho!

C. Columbus (an explorer): Coo, look everyone! America!

Of course, no one can be absolutely certain that Christopher Columbus said, 'Coo, look everyone! America!' but it is certainly the *kind* of thing he might have said. In the absence of truly knowing what he did say, neither can it be disproved!

One of the purposes behind faction is that it can make facts more digestible for the child audience for whom it is intended. To make the facts even sweeter, a lot of faction these days is couched in humorous terms. Writing a 'comic' faction version of a famous historical event or time period is very popular. Take a look around the bookshops to see what is fashionable in non-fiction.

Another example of faction would be the sort of picture book where a young child is taken for a tour of flora and fauna to be found on the seabed by a friendly, talkative and informative seahorse, crab or other character.

With children's non-fiction, the aim is always to find a new way of infiltrating information into a child's head, be it a simple 'What are Insects?' guide for very small readers or a 'Sex and Contraception' book for young adults.

In the realms of trade fiction a factual book that looks informative but light-hearted is more likely to be picked from the shelves than a dull-looking, school-like tome. Which would you choose? *Extra Maths For Beginners* or *Let's Have SUM Fun!*

A good non-fiction author has to be someone who enjoys diligent research. After all, you need to be accurate. Your publisher may not be an astronomy expert and needs to be able to trust, to a certain extent, that your inventive astronomical book is correct. Reviewers delight in finding errors in non-fiction books, and an authoritative attack on your work may kill the book's credibility and possibly damage your reputation. Your editor will also be less than amused if your location of Alpha Centauri or your certainty about the size of the sun transpire to be grossly inaccurate.

Journalists or people with a background in research often make good non-fiction authors. Interestingly enough, we have also found that very good non-fiction authors do not make good creative fiction authors and vice versa.

Humour

In children's non-fiction, as we have said, the important element is that you present your facts in an appealing way. 'Appealing' in this case has to cover several bases. A piece of work will have to appeal to teachers, librarians and parents or guardians, as well as to the child itself. It will need to be targeted accurately to the point of view of the intended age group, with suitable language, suitable interest and understanding levels, and be of a length that will deliver concisely all the necessary information in as few pages as possible. Brevity here, is very much the soul of wit, and it is a particular skill to be able to impart information in a succinct and entertaining manner.

> *All authors should make sure that their book is a children's book, not a simple adult book in disguise. The text should also be carefully aimed at the publisher's needs.*
>
> *[UK trade non-fiction publisher]*
>
> *Writing in a high-level, technical way is not appropriate. The experienced, perfect author writes few words with clarity and style – appropriate for what is required, not to impress.*
>
> *[UK educational non-fiction publisher]*

Serious, studious, sleep-inducing books are out, particularly for the trade market. 'Force-feeding' with fun is in.

Illustrations

Most modern non-fiction books will overflow with illustrations. The vast majority of information can be conveyed better with the aid of a picture, illustration, cartoon or diagram. Illustrators and designers are going to be deeply involved in the evolution of your non-fiction book right from the outset.

Your book may require photographs. There are picture libraries that keep vast collections of photographs and can probably provide a picture to go along with almost anything you might write. A designer will usually locate the appropriate pictures, but there may be occasions where this task falls to the author. Here is another fine area of time-consuming research you have gotten yourself into!

Newspapers and magazines will have their own pictorial archives which you may be able to go and plunder. Similarly, you may need to approach museums, art galleries and private collections to gather the exact source material you seek.

Obtaining permissions

Before you can reproduce any work (be it written, photographic, electronic or otherwise) permission will need to be obtained in writing from the copyright holder, payment will almost always need to be made and an acknowledgement included in the work. Before agreeing to write any commissioned, illustrated non-fiction work, check your contractual obligations with your publisher to define whose responsibility it is to obtain and pay for permissions. It is *imperative* that enough time is allowed *prior* to your book going into production for permissions to be sought and granted. Tracing the actual copyright holder of a work can be difficult and very time-consuming. However, if you do not have permission to use another's work, an expensive legal action could ensue ruining your pocket as well as your reputation.

A letter of enquiry (and as a courtesy, a self-addressed envelope) to the copyright holder should include the information about what exactly you wish to reproduce, be it text or images. You should also include details of your proposed work, its format and publication details (if you already have them).

Publishers who are the holders of copyright may reply with a form for you to complete; others may ask for further, selected details.

Sometimes, despite all your best efforts, it proves impossible to track down the copyright holder. You will sometimes see, included in the acknowledgements section of a book, wording similar to:

> Every effort has been made to trace the owners of the copyright to XXXX. It has been impossible to trace the owner and the author and publisher would be glad to hear from them.

Copyright law, particularly in regard to photographs and artworks, is a complex area. Seek advice from your publisher if you are in any doubt, or from a media copyright expert.

Checklist

Before you fling yourself into the world of non-fiction, ask yourself the following questions:

■ How good are my research skills?
■ How methodical am I?
■ How tenacious am I?
■ How accurate am I?
■ How can I make seemingly dull facts fun or interesting?

Non-fiction authors who are primarily researchers by profession or by nature can be given a theme or topic and will be able to produce an authoritative book on a subject in which they previously had little interest or knowledge.

Exercise 15

Make a list of non-fiction subjects in which you have a particular interest.

On how many of these subjects would you be willing to inject a good deal more research (meaning: exhaustive research in some cases)? Your project is going to look feeble if it turns out you have omitted an entire branch of alternative wisdom.

If you have knowledge of a particular subject, how up to date is that knowledge? In the field of computers, cutting-edge knowledge from a year ago may be blunt by now. You will also need to know what technology is under development if your work is to be as current as possible by the time it reaches the bookshops.

Difficulties

We asked a number of trade and educational non-fiction publishers to answer honestly the question, 'What percentage of your list is author inspired or editorially/in-house inspired?' Their replies are salutary!

> *Most of the list is planned here and then developed with chosen authors! Publication of unsolicited material is rare. Once authors are contracted to a project, much of the inspiration comes from them.*
>
> *Over 80 per cent of our list is in-house inspired.*
>
> *In house 80 per cent.*
>
> *Up to 90–95 per cent of our non-fiction list is conceived in-house.*
>
> *Less than 5 per cent is author inspired. Our staff editors – or freelance packaging companies – come up with most of our titles*
>
> *Almost 100 per cent in-house.*

Our next question was 'How do you find authors or contributors?' Almost every reply was similar and along these lines:

> *Agents.*
>
> *Directories, academic bodies, agents, colleagues.*
>
> *Word of mouth and personal contacts; institutions such as universities, colleges, museums, agents, occasionally unsolicited applications.*
>
> *From previous projects, by putting requests to agents, and from rejected proposals that showed ability but were rejected on the grounds of unsuitability.*

The marketplace

You may have gathered from the publishers' comments that the non-fiction market is even more difficult to break into than the fiction market! It is not easy and, like learning to ride a motorcycle, you need skill, balance, practice, perseverance and a certain amount of talent.

We next asked the same publishers if they had any words of wisdom for new authors. Every single one said the same thing: research the market and study your selected publisher's list before commencing work on a proposal. The following replies sum up the situation and offer a little more hope:

> *Do not be put off by rejection. Ninety per cent of the proposals that show some flair and ability are rejected because they are unsuitable for our list and not because they are simply awful! Study the market and think about what you are proposing. If you can show that you have thought through your ideas and investigated the market you may well be approached for some other project in the future.*

> *Whilst many of our authors come from the usual sources we also take on many authors/contributors who have written quite modest pieces/parts of books/edited etc – and are ready to develop on from there, based on past records!*

If you are an acknowledged expert in a particular field, publishers may approach you to write something or to endorse the work of others. If you already have had articles published in magazines and newspapers, this will certainly help open doors. Newspapers and magazines are good areas to consider. Periodicals are always on the lookout for new material; like television, they are great devourers of work and there is an enormous range of specialist magazines constantly needing their pages filled with new articles.

Even if these are articles are aimed at the adult reader, publishers will be impressed by the credibility attached to actually having been in print. It may be that the article could be expanded to become a children's book. This is not so unlikely as it may sound. As an expert ornithologist, you may be able to write a children's guide to birds by judiciously rethinking a published adult article.

The in-house method of creating books means that commissioning editors are always looking for authors. If you have presented a professional proposal to a suitable publisher, the editor will have your name on file. There are many reasons why your work may have been rejected, including the possibility that the publisher had already commissioned a similar project at the time yours arrived.

Presentation

Because of the nature of non-fiction works, it is not usually appropriate for an author to present a publisher with a complete, unsolicited work. The best way to present your idea is in outline form. A proposal, sample chapter and rough page-layout guide will be enough, accompanied by a polite letter of enquiry. (See Chapter 9 for details of submitting work.) We asked our non-fiction publishers whether they preferred to see proposals or completed scripts, and what they appreciated in a covering letter. The replies were yet again similar and the following are typical:

I prefer proposals and sample text – that way I have an influence over the finished ms [manuscript]. Complete scripts are usually too wide of the mark – they usually aren't tailored to the company's needs or the needs of the marketplace. Scripts should be accurately typed and come with a CV and covering letter which gives me something about background and personality. An unmemorable letter gets forgotten!

Proposals which include full contents outline and some sample text. Always helpful if author indicates what he/she considers the appropriate age-level, readership, sector of the market, rough extent and treatment of illustrations to be. And supplies a brief biography.

Proposal – stating clearly and concisely the aim, market and main strengths of the book. A sample chapter to show style and approach is useful. Personal details and relative experience is useful. Covering letter – concise, with main points only.

The wide range of non-fiction

The markets for non-fiction break down in a similar way to those for fiction: trade non-fiction books are primarily sold through traditional outlets direct to children, parents or whomever, while non-trade non-fiction finds its way into libraries, schools and other institutions.

The trade non-fiction market covers everything which is not fiction. This is broader in range than you might at first imagine: it includes puzzle books, joke books, books on how to create your own theatre, books on how to become a racing driver, and books on how to make a working origami submarine, kite-making, knot-tying, juggling, bike maintenance, how to look after a cat and a gerbil, how to extract your gerbil from your cat's mouth, first aid for cat-scratches, living with a neurotic gerbil and a homicidal moggy.

Whilst the age groupings are similar to those for the fiction market (0–3-year-olds, 3–5, 5–8, 8–12 and 12+), non-fiction books may have a much broader age-range appeal. For example, a book on fly-fishing may well be bought by a 7-year-old and a 13-year-old, as long as it is written so that it appeals to and can be understood by children of either age.

The trend in modern non-fiction is analogous to fast-food. The books have to appeal instantly to a fast-food generation, and this includes dishing out the information in easily digestible chunks as well as making it attractive to the eye. Thus, modern non-fiction books will be scattered with cartoons, jokes, information boxes, bullet points, interesting design layouts and so on. Anything, in fact, to catch the eye and interest, and hold it until money has passed hands.

Many books with non-fictional themes are presented nowadays as being fun first and knowledge second. If a book can convey useful information without the child even knowing there is a learning process in action, so much the better. Such books can deal with topics as disparate as sport, art, the lives of famous people, 'true' ghost stories, 'real-life' mysteries, interesting historical events and so on with so light a touch that even the most wilful underachiever can be hooked and reeled in.

For the older ages, say, 8+, there is also a wide variety of more text-based books with little or no illustration, covering social issues all the way from coping with grief to growing through puberty. A multitude of serious issues can be approached this way, including peer pressure, problems encountered by stepchildren, how to survive divorce or how best to approach the job-market. These books often include 'true life' stories gleaned from research with children who have encountered these things first-hand. (Research for such a book would, of course, include many interviews with these children.)

Other non-fiction is largely illustration led. A bathtime book on pond creatures may have a picture of a fish with the single word, 'fish', underneath. Or a backyard book could have a picture of a wriggly worm accompanied by the word, 'worm', and similar pages for spiders, centipedes, beetles and a yeti. (Well, maybe not a yeti, unless your backyard happens to be halfway up a mountain in the Himalayas.)

Cookery books for children can form the other end of this illustrated genre. The book may explain the ingredients, recipe and cooking methods with simple text accompanied by large, colour photographs showing what the child's sticky brown wreck of a soufflé should really look like when it emerges from the oven.

You could even write an illustrated book on how to make your own illustrated book. And the illustrated book you might be making from your illustrated instruction book might even be an illustrated instruction book on how to make your own illustrated book!

As with illustrated fiction books, these illustrated non-fiction works are very costly to produce and a lot of the comments included in Chapter 6 are pertinent here. Publishers will be very selective about what they produce because of the cost of commissioning artwork, photographs, picture research and designers. Trade publishers in particular will be on the lookout for something with an international appeal, something that will suit as many different countries and cultures as possible, so it may be as well not to be too parochial when you present your proposal.

This is not to say that a publisher would automatically dismiss a book exploring the flora and fauna of a particular country or region, or a book which explores that country or region's traditions or politics. Such books have a place in the non-fiction market – they may just be a little harder to sell in large quantities. On the other hand a well-produced book on the Sahara Desert or the Florida Everglades is more likely to find a worldwide audience and provide plenty of profit.

Payment

Many non-fiction authors are paid a flat fee or a one-off payment for their text work. This is because their input is seen as just one element in a complex production process. They are not generally viewed as the 'author' of the work but as a single contributor.

Hence, advances and royalties are less forthcoming from non-fiction publishers than they would be in the fiction world. (Something else to bear in mind before you head off for a six-month research trek across Siberia.)

Educational publishers

Specialist educational publishers produce books mainly for the school and library markets, so they will be seeking projects which are invariably educationally linked. If you are interested in this field, you will need to find out what children are studying and at what age, so that books can be pitched appropriately. For instance, if children study ancient China only between the ages of 7 and 8 in your country, there is little purpose in preparing an educationally-based proposal on this subject for 13-year-olds. No one will want it.

Books produced by educational publishers range from history to art, from science to social issues, from mathematics to special needs, from drama to literature, and all points in between. They will include books providing interesting information: technical know-how from photography to mechanics to quantum physics.

These books will include companion websites, photocopiable teaching aids, beginner readers, dictionaries, study books, encyclopedias and CD-ROMs. (Incidentally, these photocopiable teaching aids are the only books from which it is strictly legal for teachers to copy pages for their pupils to take away for homework or to use for set tasks in school time.) The law on photocopying is a little grey in places. If you want to know the facts, you know what to do ... research!

Non-fiction multimedia ranges from learning a foreign language to how-to-draw packages, from encyclopedias to interactive games, and so on.

Essentially, you must take a long look at your skills and carefully consider how best to use them. Those of you with teaching experience will find that this scores highly with a commissioning editor, assuming your projected book falls within the parameters of your expertise.

Publishers' pet hates

We asked the non-fiction publishers what their pet hate were. These included:

> *Ill-considered proposals, people who 'cold-call' wanting to discuss their project at length over the phone.*

> *Writing in a high-level, technical way when not appropriate. Writing too many words, even after an editorial briefing! Unreliability. Lack of clarity. We also never bring together authors who don't know each other and automatically expect them to work well together. So – if the author of a submission can work well with a co-author, suggest it.*

> *Authors who draw their own pictures, or naively think they have to do all the artwork and take all the photos themselves.*

And if you still have not received and understood our main message, take heed from this patient publisher:

> *I will give a lot more attention to letters from people who have bothered to find out what we publish. I get irritated by people who haven't done the slightest bit of research before they write. Unrealistic proposals are a complete waste of time.*

> *I received a two-line letter from someone who was proposing to write a history of Britain. The two lines contained four spelling mistakes (including the writer's address). The accompanying proposal comprised a box (in which I was supposed to imagine a picture of George III) and four bullet points of four or five words each about George IV. There was no CV, and no other clue to the author's identity. Nothing. Would I give any time to someone who treated such a huge project so feebly? Of course not!*

Schedules are often very rigid in children's non-fiction, with very heavy initial investment costs. When an author doesn't deliver the goods, it's extremely painful. Most editors will therefore tend to turn to the authors they know and trust rather than try out new names who might not deliver what's wanted on time. What this means is that unsolicited material gets a lot less attention than it does in other areas of publishing. It doesn't take much to consign a proposal to the dustbin.

Co-authoring

You may be asked to co-author a work of non-fiction with one or more other authors. Occasionally, fiction books are co-authored and these can present more problems than non-fiction: rarely can you establish an exact division on who did what. One author invariably thinks they have produced 51 per cent of the work and their colleague, 49 per cent. On non-fiction, it may be easier to define the share of work. When it comes to dividing up the money, authors can fall out with each other permanently. Before agreeing to co-author any work, try to establish the boundaries in advance. Your editor may be able to mediate. The same applies if you are asked to 'ghost write' a work – perhaps for a blind author who cannot key in text, or for a famous person who created a storyline idea but who cannot actually write children's books (in which case, their name is really being used on the cover as a selling feature).

Checklist

Before beginning work, and before you submit that non-fiction proposal you should follow these steps towards success:

1. Find a theme, topic, or original or unusual subject.
2. Approach it from an interesting angle.
3. Decide upon your style, be it humorous, serious or whatever.
4. Get the whole thing onto paper: outline, sample chapter or suggested layout.
5. Seek out an appropriate publisher.

6. Send the proposal off along with a polite, brief yet informative letter of enquiry, and your biographical details.

7. While you are waiting for a response, do not just sit there: get to work on another idea!

9 | PRESENTATION AND SUBMISSION OF WORK

Luck or judgement?

It is not *what* you know, but *who* you know that counts. Well, that is true enough. Knowing the right people can be very helpful in opening life's more securely fastened doors. But even if your grandparents own a publishing house, are members of the landed gentry and drink their martinis shaken, not stirred, with the jet set, it does not automatically follow that *you* are going to produce a bestseller. Getting into the business involves a little more than a fortunate birth; you cannot leave it all to luck. You need to sell yourself a little, within reason.

So you are champing at the bit to get your work published. You are invited to a party and happen to bump into someone who is involved in the world of publishing and who seems to you likely to be a useful contact. Do you accost this individual and force your ideas on them for the rest of the evening?

No, you don't!

Heed this advice from a weary publisher:

> Don't *talk about projects at social occasions; ask for a name and address/card.*
>
> Don't *then ring up the office – write.*

A dialogue

> *The scene*: A supermarket checkout. A person with many years' experience in children's publishing is waiting in line to pay for their week's shopping. A hopeful author happens to have found out what this person does for a living, and sees the chance to advance their cause!

The characters: Anne Eddittorre and Hope ffulle-Author.

(Hope ffulle-Author shoves her way through the line of shoppers)

HffA: Hello, there. My name is Hope ffulle-Author. This is your lucky day – I've written a brilliant book that will make us all rich.

AE: Ye-es ... uh, is it a book for children?

HffA: Well, it's got a message for everyone, really. Everyone from 8 to 80. Ninety, even!

AE: I take it it's fiction. How long is the story?

HffA: It's sort of fiction, and non-fiction, really. The story revolves around my lovely old dog Bozo who sadly died a couple of months ago. We've had him stuffed and mounted in the hall if you'd like to come around and see him some time. Anyway the really brilliant thing is that I've come up with this stunningly original concept where Bozo can speak! Fantastic, huh? And he can fly and do just about everything. In Chapter 6 he single-pawedly solves all the ecological problems of the entire planet and discovers how to make sure everyone loves everyone else. In the *nicest* way, of course. No smut, you know. And then he flies off into outer space in search of the almigh ...

AE (politely but firmly interrupting): I see. Sounds interesting. How long would you say the script was?

HffA: Uh, I don't know. I haven't actually finished typing it out yet or anything. But my writing is really easy to read. I mean, take no notice of my partner – they say I write like a dyslexic spider in boxing gloves. It's just not true. My next door neighbour is a doctor, and she says she can read nearly every word. And she thinks it's brilliant. Anyway, the book is about 234 pages long so far and still going strong. Would you like to read some of it? As it's the weekend, I don't suppose you'll have much on, so I could get the first 12 notebooks over to you later this afternoon, if you like. No problem.

(Sound of Anne slumping to the floor)

HffA: Oh dear, she seems to have fainted. It must be the excitement! Help! Call an ambulance, somebody!

This scene could also take place in line for the drinks at a party, in a crowded lift or in the office of an editor who forgets to put his voice-mail answering machine on, and unsuspectingly picks up the ringing telephone. It need not be an editor on the receiving end, either. It could be anyone whom Hope ffulle-Author happens to know is involved in some way in children's books. In ten years' time it could be you!

A letter

The following is a hypothetical letter sent to a publishing house from another eager author. This time, a Mr Ivan E. Normusego writes:

Dear Sir or MAdam

I have looked at all the meterial avaliable for chidlren and a lot of i'ts at the best unsuitable and at wort itter grabage, I no i can do much better ans so i wrote a series of books about a little school bu called Mister Toot-Sweet dn all the fantastical going on he comes acorss in his erevyday journies. I have reed it to my next door neigfhbour who is a supermarket manger and nobodies' fool, and he says its a sur-fire woinner and I going to get Mister_Toot sweat trademarked and the quartersize salt-dough model I have made also patented,

I also see Mister Toot-Sweet as a cartoon which Dizney could animate and also it has a million marketting and merchandising pissibilities!!!

This idea miust be treated in the strictest confidense and i await your reply by return of post otherwise i shall take it to someone else and then youl'l be sorry..

Your sincerey

Ivan E. Normusego

Are we exaggerating? Unfortunately not: the above are fairly realistic examples of the sort of incompetent, unthought-out approaches that the worst would-be authors make to people in the world of children's books all the time. If you listen carefully you might be able to hear, at this very moment, the screams of an editor as they run down an office corridor tearing their hair out in despair.

The chances that Hope or Ivan will get their work into print are slim, to be honest.

In a competitive market like children's publishing, you have to give thought to *presentation*. You cannot wrap a bad idea up in pretty paper and get it through the net – but you can make a good idea *better* if you take the right approach.

Let us go back and take a look at exactly what those two would-be authors did wrong. It might help if you go over both examples again before you read on. Make notes of where you think they went haywire, and of what approach *should* have been employed.

Hope ffulle-Author

Timing

Everyone knows the story of the professional comedian approached by some idiot at a party and asked to tell a joke. 'What do *you* do for a living?' retorts the comedian. 'I'm a plumber,' comes the reply. 'Okay, then,' says the comedian. 'Let's see you fix a ball-cock.'

Hope ffulle-Author has done something similar to the idiot party guest by assaulting Anne Eddittorre out of working hours. The very least you should do is to approach professional people at their place of work and within working hours, including those who work from home full or part time. The alternative is simply rude.

Age range

Not many books are read by people of all ages. Children's books may be read by adults to children, or reread by adults who remember them with affection from their own childhood, or even read by adults because the book touches the child's heart in everyone.

On the whole, children's books will fit into specific age-range categories. The fact that Hope imagines that her book will be read universally suggests very strongly that she knows virtually nothing about the market. She probably has not even *read* a children's book for years, let alone taken the trouble to investigate libraries, bookshops or to make contact with any children at all since she waved goodbye to the old school gates in her teens. Had she done so, she may have noticed the curious lack of enormously lengthy stories about dead dogs who go around saving the universe. She might have spotted that children simply *hate* books that shove a really obvious message down their throats. Children do not want books that are good for them. They want books which are *fun*.

Hope has not even finished her book, let alone typed it all up. In fact, she has no clear idea of how long her book is or how long it will end up being. She also makes another big mistake. Suppose she really does have a good idea going, a totally brilliant idea. The very last thing she should be doing is telling all and sundry before her idea is in a finished and presentable form.

There are several reasons for keeping a good idea to yourself. 'Ideas' once they have been aired have the strange tendency to resurface elsewhere and be written by someone else. It is a bit like the reeds whispering that Midas has asses ears. We are not suggesting that ideas are intentionally stolen, but such things can lie dormant in someone else's brain and then emerge from the subconscious as if from nowhere. There is a familiar phenomenon in the publishing world whereby several stories or proposals on virtually the same subject, by authors who have never met, will land on an editor's desk in the same week.

If you have a good idea, just jot it down, keep it private, and only discuss it with people you trust. Hope ffulle-Author would be very put-out if her doctor neighbour had a book published called Bozo the Superdog, but she might not be able to do anything about it. (We will cover safeguarding your work later.)

Ivan E. Normusego

Addressee

Ivan has not taken the trouble to find out to whom he should be addressing his letter. In fact, for all Ivan knows, he could have made contact with a publisher who deals solely with Russian-to-English translations of sewage plant equipment manuals.

Spelling and typing: Ivan cannot spell. Not all writers can spell, but there are dictionaries, spell-checkers on computers and even dinky little electronic gizmos to help you out, as well as literate friends or colleagues. Nor can Ivan type. Everyone allows the odd 'typo' (typing or typographical error) to slip through, but there is no excuse for anyone to send a letter that looks like someone has spilt a can of alphabet spaghetti onto a sheet of paper and then sealed it in an envelope.

It would be very clear to whoever receives this 'communication' from Ivan that he has not even bothered to reread his own letter and, to be brutally honest, that he is probably several chapters short of a bestseller! As we said before, presentation is vitally important. It is part of your professional approach.

The market

Ivan says he has taken a good look at the market for which the book is intended, but his observations are made clearly from a very biased point of view. Anyone who blithely proclaims that everything available to children is 'garbage' does not have a very objective view of things.

He should also bear in mind that the opinions of family, friends and neighbours are usually of limited value. The supermarket manager, in thinking Mister Toot-Sweet would be a money-spinner, might be right. Then again, he is just as likely to be wrong. The fact is that unless your family, friends and neighbours are involved in publishing, their opinion has no real weight. You should also bear in mind that people from whom you seek opinions are unlikely to tell you that your beloved project is utterly ghastly. These people are more likely to be polite to you, and will usually tell you what they think you want to hear:

A very common statement in submission letters is '... I've shown it to all my friends and they think it's great'. Well they would wouldn't they? My boss once said that he would love to get a proposal from someone which started 'I've shown it to all my friends and they all think it's a load of rubbish, but I still think it's a good idea'. At least then you'd feel you were getting something original, something the author really believed in.

[Publisher of children's trade non-fiction]

Expectations

As with most occupations and experiences, it is handy to have learnt to walk before you enter a marathon. Maybe Ivan's idea *would* make an amazing special-effects movie; and possibly children throughout the world would stampede over their own grandparents to get at a Mister Toot-Sweet pencil case. First and foremost, however, Hope's and Ivan's ideas should be seen as *books*. The spin-offs would come later on, if at all, and a prospective publisher is unlikely to be overexcited by the grandiose merchandising concepts of either budding author.

Know the publishing style and philosophy of a house before you submit your work; you can get a sense of this by requesting a publisher's catalogs and by reading the books they publish. If your work doesn't suit a particular house, don't submit it; find a publisher that's compatible with your style. Be selective and target your submissions carefully.

[US publisher]

Research publisher's lists through bookshops, libraries, catalogues, to discover if the project is likely to be suitable for them before sending it off. Also research the competition and consider how your project would/could stand up to it. With non-fiction, try to understand the difference between an educational list and a non-fiction trade list.

[English / French publisher]

Authors help themselves a great deal if they first try to find out what a particular publisher actually publishes. Show them that you chose their house because you know and like them. And that you've given it some effort to find out.

The above quote comes from a French publisher, but reflects the feeling of every publisher we contacted.

Forgive us for labouring and reiterating various points, but you want to write children's books *and* get them published. You should by now be nearly ready to draft your submission letter and put together your precious package of work. Before doing that, consider the following small situation:

The scene: an interview room for a Very Important Merchant Bank. Three Very Important People sit behind a long desk looking Very Important. In front of the desk is a solitary chair.

(Knock on door)

Chief interviewer (to his colleagues): Ah, that will be Miss Burglebrain, who seemed from her written responses to be the ideal candidate for the job we have on offer. She is charismatic, charming, intelligent, go-getting, capable, painstaking and a leading member of Mensa. *(Aloud)* Enter!

(Enter Miss Burglebrain)

(She is wearing a tutu, wellington boots, a fireman's helmet and a half-metre-long nose which revolves and sprays cocoa)

Miss Burglebrain: Hello, everyone. Is it okay to bring my pet skunk in?

Chief interviewer: NEXT APPLICANT!

What did Miss Burglebrain do wrong? She packaged herself very badly. Despite being charismatic, charming and all the rest, she presented herself as being several islands short of an archipelago. She gave herself no chance to prove whether she would have been any good in the job or not.

Miss Burglebrain was her own worst enemy, and you must not put yourself into the same position. When your work lands on a publisher's desk, make sure that you have given it the best publishing chance possible. Good presentation of your material is absolutely vital.

You want, via your presented work, to be seen as a professional author, not someone for whom writing is a kind of hobby.

The typescript

Example

Partners in Crime series   Book One

In At the Deep End

What could she do? Eddie Stone was in control – any action she took would imperil both of them. Unless she could jump clear while they were over the water.

She moved her hand to the door.

'Central locking, Maddie,' Eddie said calmly. 'You won't be able to get it open. Sorry.'

A kind of wild desperation flowed through Maddie. For a few crazy moments she didn't care what happened to her – she just had to do something to silence his voice – something that would hurt him as much as his family had hurt her.

She jack-knifed her legs, bunching her muscles and twisting in her seat. She kicked out towards the dashboard with both feet. She had no thought in her head other than the desire to bring the helicopter down and put an end to this whole terrible ordeal.

Eddie let out a shout of alarm and anger as Maddie's feet smashed into the controls of the helicopter. But he was too late. The damage had been done.

The turbine engine Jetranger helicopter has a switch-off valve – a red switch located on the bank in front of the pilot. It cuts off the fuel. The heel of Maddie's right foot came hammering down on the red switch —engaging it and breaking it off in one movement. Sparks fizzed and flew from the control panel.

'You stupid fool!' Eddie wrenched at the joystick. The helicopter shuddered and began to keel over in the air. The engine was starved of fuel. The rotors began to slow.

'Don't take it personally, Eddie.' Maddie's eyes were cold. 'It was just a business decision.'

1

Note: the above page is reproduced from an unedited typescript for the Partners in Crime series by Allan Frewin Jones.

Your typescript (which is often called a 'manuscript' in the publishing world) must be presented professionally. The actual layout is acceptable in slightly varying formats, but the sample page given shows you the basic idea.

White paper

Your manuscript must be on white A4 paper. The paper should be of reasonable quality. Do not use any kind of thin, easily-torn or damaged paper, as these will look a total mess after one or two read-throughs. Do not use expensive, heavyweight paper either, as it will cost a fortune to send through the mail and may well be wasted if the manuscript needs to be heavily rewritten (a likelihood you should always keep in mind). You could end up spending a lot of money needlessly. Your best bet may be to seek the advice of a stationer as to an ideal paper weight and type. Some people find that standard photocopying paper does the job perfectly well.

Black print

Your manuscript must be printed in black ink. This photocopies better than any other colour, as well as generally being easier on the eye. Choose a typeface of a size and style which is easy to read, such as Times New Roman, **Helvetica**, `Courier` or similar; 12pt is the best size to use. If you are working on a computer, be sure not to use draft printouts for your final presentation copy. Ensure that your ink or toner is printing clearly.

Layout

The layout of a page is all-important and pretty much standard throughout the publishing world. Use double-spacing: this means you must leave a full line gap between every line of print. Also be sure to leave wide margins on either side of the text and at the top and the bottom of the page.

Wide margins and double-spacing have an entirely practical purpose. It is to allow a copy-editor enough room to make notes and alterations and to write down instructions to the typesetter/ printer, which usually will be done in red or sometimes blue ink, which will stand out from the black type. (Now you see why sending a manuscript in coloured ink is a potentially confusing idea.)

TY Children's Books   168

In general, the text should have a straight margin on the
left (ranged left this is called). It should not be
"justified". A "justified" script is one where there are
straight down both the left-hand and right-hand sides of the
script, as in a book. An unjustified script looks much
like a more widely spaced business letter. If you are
working on computer, do not "justify" your script as this
may cause confusion for the typesetters later on.

You should leave one blank space after the full stop,
comma, semi-colon or colon and the beginning of the next. Don't use
"bold" print for emphasis or italics, but simply
underline words you wish stressed or put them into
CAPITALS.

You may have been taught to indent new paragraphs and
dialogue (i.e., leave five letter spaces before starting
a fresh paragraph or piece of dialogue.) This is no
longer strictly necessary as a copy-editor will alter the
layout to suit their requirements. Publishers prefer a one-line
gap between paragraphs.
Likewise,
However, each new piece of dialogue in a conversation
should be given a fresh line. It looks better on the page
and makes it easier to follow the conversation than would
be the case if it was all strung together in a single
paragraph. dialogue

Every new chapter should be started on a fresh page.
[LESLEY: CRIKEY! REALLY? YOU NEVER TOLD ME THAT.] This

Delete!

The copy-editor, by the way, is the person who makes all the alterations and corrections in the code understood by typesetters. We have bravely included opposite a page of our second draft script, from this chapter, which was patiently edited by our long-suffering friend, and freelance editor, Iain Brown.

If you compare this page with the final printed one in this chapter, you will see how a copy-editor will work on your script, making suggestions for improving the text and drawing the author's attention to anything that may be confusing or unclear to a reader. Unfortunately, however often a script is read and revised, there is still a time when you have to stop. (For all our care, and that of the production process, no doubt you will still find typographical errors and omissions in this book.)

The title page of your manuscript should include the title of the work and your name or the pseudonym under which you would like the work to be published. It should also include your address, telephone and fax numbers, and e-mail address. If you are represented by an agent, then their name and address should be included on the title page in place of your address. Also provide the word-count of the script; that is, how long it is (most computers now have a word-count facility). There is no need to add a copyright or a serial rights line. (We shall go into copyrighting your work later in this chapter.)

One thing you should *never* do is to date the manuscript, as it may have to pass through the hands of several publishers before it finds a home. Each stopping-off point could mean a sojourn of several weeks (or even months), and any printed date will help the publisher work out that she is not the first to have seen it. This is not a good idea if you want a positive response!

The moment your script starts to show its age, it will lose a good deal of its initial appeal. Hence the use of reasonable quality paper that will survive a few readings, and your avoidance of anything that will show it has 'done the rounds'. Your content must also be reasonably timeless, so a reminder here that this year's pop star, news item and 'buzzword' may be meaningless by the time your work gets into print.

Text for typescripts and discs

Many scripts are now delivered both in 'hard copy' (printed on paper) and on disc. Once your work has found a home you can check your contract or ask your editor for details of what they require (they may accept commissioned material via e-mail). Many publishers also have briefs on how to submit final work. In general, the text should have a straight margin on the left ('ranged left' this is called). It should not be 'justified'. A 'justified' script is one where there are straight edges down both the left-hand and right-hand sides of the script, as in a book. If you are working on computer, do not 'justify' your script as this may cause confusion for the typesetters.

You should leave one blank character space after a full stop or any punctuation mark, unlike common business letter practice. Do not use 'bold' print for emphasis or italics, but simply <u>underline</u> words you wish stressed. Avoid any fancy type (font) styles, too.

You may have been taught to indent new paragraphs and dialogue (that is, leave five character spaces before starting a fresh paragraph or piece of dialogue). This is no longer strictly necessary as a copy-editor will alter the layout to suit their requirements. Publishers prefer a one-line gap between paragraphs. Likewise, each new piece of dialogue in a conversation should be given a fresh line. It distinguishes it from the prose on the page and makes the conversation easier to follow.

Every new chapter should be started on a fresh page. This fresh page should include the chapter number and its title (if it has one).

Your computer should have a header and footer facility. It is a good idea to use it, to save loose pages getting entirely lost: all you need to do is include your name and the book title. In this way, pages that go astray can easily be returned to the fold.

Page numbering

Page numbering is absolutely, totally and completely *vital*. The pages of your manuscript must be numbered consecutively right through the book. In other words, the first page should be '1' and the one-hundred-and-thirtieth page should be '130'. Do not number new chapters afresh. Follow the numbering sequence right through.

The page numbers should be located either centrally at the bottom of every manuscript page, or in the top right-hand corner. If you are three-quarters of the way through a script and have forgotten to add page numbers, do not despair. There is nothing wrong with adding them by hand, but do it soon. An open window and a stiff breeze could result in a full day spent sorting out an unnumbered script.

An experienced editor will also be able to roughly judge the length of your work by looking at the number of the final page – if you have not included a word-count on the title page.

As well as typing services, there are also 'criticism' services available if you would like an 'in-the-know' outside eye to be run over your work before you present it to a publisher. It may be beneficial to have an objective viewpoint to edit, tidy up and make constructive suggestions on your work. This service, as well as that of typists, can be found through various author associations and magazines, but compare prices and use a recommended service if possible.

Fiction synopses

You may wish to include a synopsis of your fiction book along with the manuscript. This can be a good and a bad thing. A busy publisher may read the synopsis in preference to the book, but what if the synopsis does not appeal and therefore he/she decides to investigate no further? Your well-presented manuscript fails by default. On the other hand, an exciting story given in a well-written précis may make a publisher persevere with a book which has not riveted them early on in the text. It is your decision, but if you do decide to include a synopsis for a story which has an unexpected ending or 'twist', then do not give the final game away by clearly stating the details. Allow your editor to be surprised.

If you are not submitting a full manuscript, then a publisher will need to see a well-written synopsis of the basic plot as well as the three opening chapters of the book; or possibly the first chapter and then two sample chapters which you think are particularly exciting or representative. These chapters will not only show your writing ability, but will prove you have the wherewithal to actually produce a finished book. The synopsis, incidentally, should not be shorter than half a page, and could be considerably longer in a complex novel – but do not get carried away: the job of the synopsis is to present the story in as brief a way as the weight of the plot will allow.

Non-fiction manuscripts

The title page for a non-fiction manuscript should be the same as outlined above, but you should also give an idea of the type of material contained in the manuscript. Explain what it is that you are proposing to convey and to whom it is targeted (the latter information should by now be to hand if you have been following our guidelines). For example:

> *Edible Bookmarks for Beginners* (working title), a proposal aimed at the 5–7 year age group on how to make, bake and create bookmarks which can be eaten.

You can decide exactly how to lay out your title page, but if you have a computer then you can use a large typeface for the main title, and centre it on the page.

What to include

A contents page would help to give a quick impression of your book. Include chapter headings with perhaps a sentence or two about the material contained in each chapter. Remember that it is not a good idea to submit completed material. It may turn out to be the same as another recently published work, or possibly your ideas may suit a publisher whilst your style does not. Thus a synopsis will give you the opportunity to present your ideas and allow a prospective publisher to guide you in the actual writing of the book so that it fits in with the house style. This could save you having to write the book twice!

Your proposal or synopsis outline could also include any marketing ideas you may have for selling your book. Potential sales areas for *Edible Bookmarks for Beginners* would include the usual trade and non-trade markets, but might appeal to foodstores, with a promotional link to a particular product or range of products. The more innovative yet practical ideas you can suggest, the more your publisher will know that you have done your homework, and the more they may be convinced that yours is a viable project. (We shall expand on marketing and promotion in Chapter 12.) You will also need to include a sample chapter, or some example page layouts of your proposed work.

Illustrations

If photographs or illustrations are integral to the book, then send photocopies, preferably on A4 paper, to give the script a well-packaged look. Colour copies or printouts can be produced easily and cheaply these days. Remember what we said in the previous chapter about getting permission to use photographs and art? If such permission has been obtained, send copies of the permission documentation, too.

Should you have a very specific idea for the layout of your work (if it is to be highly illustrated, for example), then send in a design plan to the publisher. This can be done by using some A3 paper (420 mm × 297 mm, the size of two A4 sheets placed side by side), folding it in two and then showing the proposed design for a typical spread. In this case, text could be typed or *neatly* handwritten with copies or hand-drawn illustration layout suggestions ('roughs'). It does not matter if you are not an artist, or are not planning to illustrate the book yourself, simple drawings may well be enough to convey your meaning.

Think very carefully before submitting unsolicited original illustrations. At the very least, they may well be out of your hands for several months; at worst, they could get lost somewhere in the deeper recesses of the underground catacombs of a postal sorting office and be eaten by a family of hungry rats.

Even if peckish rodents are kept at bay by the diligence of postal employees, your precious illustrations could still get battered, knocked about and trodden on, and have coffee spilled on them, or simply disappear between publisher's offices. In that case, even the usual ritual slaughter of an office junior will not bring your illustrations back. Colour photocopying may seem expensive, but in this case, the financial outlay will at least ensure a sound night's sleep untroubled by the faint scrabble of claws and subterranean chewing noises.

Author/illustrators of all work

If you are an author/illustrator familiar with the technicalities of producing an illustrated children's book (as explained in Chapter 6), then you can go about presenting your work in one of several ways. If you have completed the artwork, then you could submit colour photocopies, numbered to correspond to the script. If colour photocopying the entire book proves prohibitively expensive, a better option may be to submit one or two colour copies of those illustrations in which you have the greatest faith, and the rest could then be copied in black and white. (Publishers' abbreviation for black and white is 'B/W' or 'B&W', by the way.)

You may wish possibly to present a 'dummy' book, by which we mean a mock-up of your book showing the page layouts, style, size and even examples of any paper engineering if the book is intended to include cut-outs or additions. Such a dummy book can range from a stapled-together booklet executed in pencil, to an A4 page of simple sketches or a 'zig-zag', which is a length of paper folded concertina-like. We are not going into great detail on this, because if you do not know what we mean, you probably should not be submitting your own artwork!

The full manuscript

As a result of all your hard work and study, you now have a completed manuscript in front of you. What do you do next? Well, what you certainly do not do is to hole-punch it, ring-bind it, staple it chapter by chapter, paperclip bits of it together, tie it up in string, arc-weld it, nail it to a plank or do anything else to it at all. Your manuscript must be left *loose-leaf*, no matter how uneasy that makes you feel. Your book is almost guaranteed to pass through several pairs of hands. Punched holes can easily tear under frequent manipulation; the paper will show creases, curls and scuffs from being folded over staples; and any kind of binding will speed the deterioration in the look of the script. They are also time-consuming for a busy editor to struggle with. Many editors can and will speed read a submission. Clips and bindings slow that process down and can annoy, and you do not want to do anything to upset your prospective publisher, do you?

Simply put the manuscript in page order, give it a quick shuffle and thump to make it look neat and tidy, and slip a couple of elastic bands around it. Two elastic bands side to side and two top to bottom should do the trick; ensuring that your manuscript stays together in transit and maintains its pristine loveliness. Place your manuscript in a simple cardboard folder of a snug size which will fit into, usually, an A4 padded envelope. (Illustrations can be sent in an A3 size package, but be very wary of sending a publisher anything too large: enormous great packages will not find easy accommodation on a desk, and who knows where it may be slipped temporarily so as to be out of the way, and then forgotten.) For additional security you could add card sleeves to either end of your manuscript before placing it in the folder.

On the outside of the folder, write your name or pseudonym, your address, the title of the work and, this time, the date of submission. Why date it when we were so adamant that the manuscript itself should have no date? It is simply that a date on the folder may well remind the recipient that it is high time they read the manuscript. If the work is returned, the folder can be replaced with a new one, or if it is in good condition the information can be covered with a label with a new date on it. Hey presto! Instant contemporaneity!

The title

It is not vital for your work to have a definite title at this point: it could have a 'working title', which is a word or phrase by which you can identify it – *The Earwig That Flew*, for instance. In this case, write on the folder: THE EARWIG THAT FLEW (working title for 32 pp children's story) by Ikan Tell. In the case of non-fiction, PIRACY FOR BEGINNERS – proposal idea for 7–11-year-olds, by Aaargh Jimlad.

Before you settle on a final title, be sure to check that it is *original*. There is basically no copyright in titles (trademarking of original typography is an exception), but it would be plain daft to select a famous published title or one previously chosen by half a dozen other people. On the other hand, it is not worth agonizing over a title at this stage, especially as your publisher may have their own astute ideas as to what your work should be called.

Submission letters

Your proposal is prepared, packaged and ready to go in the post to your chosen publisher.

You may have found your publisher's address from an annual writer's reference book or website. This is as good a place to start as any, but the speed with which things change in the world of publishing could mean that an incumbent in the New Year may be history by May. The safest thing, if you have any doubt about your information, is to telephone the publisher and ask the receptionist the name of the senior commissioning editor. Be certain to ask for the name of the editor in the particular field in which you are interested. Large publishing houses are split into many departments; make certain you have been given the name of the right person. 'Could you give me the name of the editor in charge of children's non-fiction, please?' will do the trick. If, for some reason, the receptionist is unable to help you, they may put you through to someone in the appropriate department. Do not use this as an opportunity to buttonhole an editor: it will not go down well. Briefly, politely and professionally ask for the name you need, and check the spelling and title (Mr, Mrs or Ms) if you are at all unsure.

Of course, if someone asks you why you are enquiring, then by all means give a very brief outline, but do not treat this as a pre-interview, or you will become like Hope ffulle-Author!

The submission letter is possibly the most important item in your package. It can instantly enchant or antagonize the recipient. Thus, it must be well written; it must be professional.

All the publishers we contacted with our questionnaire, both fiction and non-fiction and from all over the world, said precisely the same: that they want to receive typescripts and proposals in hard copy, in the manner we have described, and never just a computer disc alone or by e-mail. *All* the publishers said they did not want telephone calls describing your work at length. *All* said that they did not wish to receive original or amateur artwork. *All* agreed on what they do and do not like to see in a submission letter. The following two responses are typical:

Badly written letters, or proposals containing poor spelling and punctuation get rejected. If a writer is incapable of checking an introductory letter then there's precious little chance that he/she is going to take care over a manuscript.

[Non-fiction publisher]

Covering letters should be kept as brief and to the point as possible. It's easier to say what I do not appreciate in them:

a) I do not want the author's life history.

b) I do not want to know that several kids next door/their son's class at school or whoever think this is the best book ever written.

c) I certainly do not want emotional blackmail. It makes me uncomfortable and annoyed if I get letters telling me that the author has recently been made redundant/has multiple sclerosis/suffers from depression. I've had all these more than once.

[Fiction publisher]

Type or print your letter on good quality white paper, preferably A4, and with a legible, standard typeface (do avoid handwritten letters). The letter *must* include (at the top) your name, address, telephone and/or fax number, e-mail address (if you have one) and date.

Begin the letter, 'Dear Ed Spearance', or 'Dear Ms Spearance'. Do not start the letter 'Dear Ed' or 'Hi Ed' unless you know the editor personally. Similarly, do not start off with anything like 'Hello, there, I saw you speak at the So-and-so conference, and darned good you were too, as I said to the person sitting next to me at the time'.

Start your letter by giving a very brief explanation of the material you are submitting, include its title (in capitals or italics so that it stands out) and a very small amount of relevant information about yourself, include any previous successes you have had in getting into print. In the case of a non-fiction work, give appropriate background information about yourself to reinforce the recipient's understanding of why have written the book. Endeavour to keep to one page (if it is more than one, paperclip it together) and attach it to your folder with another elastic band.

Everyone is different

Your submission letter will probably need to be adjusted every time you send a script to a different publisher, for varying reasons. Some editors who responded to our questionnaires said that they like memorable letters. We have seen some very amusing (to us) submission letters which made the recipients respond favourably. We have also seen some very unamused responses to the same letters. If you have heard an editor give a talk at a conference, you may have a better idea of that editor's personality. Use your best judgement.

Confidentiality

Because of the very nature of the relationship between authors and publishers, you can consider that your work is submitted in complete confidence. If your project is especially innovative, then it will be as well to include in your letter a confidentiality sentence: 'This typescript is submitted to you in confidence' is sufficient. We do not recommend that you use this on every submission, as it can come across as a little pretentious on a standard project. However, if you do truly believe that you have created the next world best-selling idea (but be realistic about this), find a media copyright expert and ask them to draw up a letter of confidentiality. You will of course have to pay such experts, but sadly it is not unheard of for projects (usually for the adult trade book area) to have been 'stolen'. The letter of confidentiality will be sent to, and signed by the prospective recipient before you deliver any material. These letters are more commonly submitted in connection with material which may be libellous or controversial, something we do not normally expect to see in connection with children's books.

Return postage

You must include sufficient stamps to cover the return postage of your package if the publisher rejects it. (Yes, *rejects* it. A nasty word, 'rejects', but you will need to get used to it – see the next chapter.) Mention in your letter that return postage has been included and then tuck the stamps securely under the paperclip. Remember that we are talking about unsolicited manuscripts here.

Why should a publisher feel obliged to pay for the return postage on a manuscript they did not ask you to send? Better still, include a stamped, self-addressed label or envelope. (If possible, get yourself an up-to-date copy of postal rates and an accurate set of scales so that you can weigh your package at home and put the appropriate number of stamps inside. Should you have to go to the post office to find out what the postage will be, leave the package open and take some sticky tape with you so you can insert the stamps and then seal the package rather than having to take it all the way back home again.)

You could also include a stamped, self-addressed acknowledgement card, which on one side has the name of the publisher and a line saying 'We acknowledge safe receipt of A BUCKET OF SLUDGE by Pete Bog, dated ...'. Some publishers do not automatically send out such cards, and you do want to know that your package has arrived safely. (Of course you do: remember the rats at the sorting office?)

Keep a copy! Keep a copy!

Never, ever, under any circumstances send off your one and only original copy of a manuscript. If you are working with a computer, you should make a second 'hard' copy and also save your work to a floppy disc. (A 'hard' copy just means a 'real' copy on real paper in real ink, as opposed to an 'electronic' copy on your computer disc.) It is not outrageously expensive these days, and it is absolutely vital. It would be quite insane of you to commit your only copy to the postal service or to a publisher. Publishers cannot be held responsible for the disappearance of your manuscript, and although the post office may be held liable for things that go astray in their hands (if proven), no compensation is going to make up for the absolute loss of many months' hard work.

There is no real need for you to go to the additional expense of insuring or registering your package. If you have addressed it clearly, put sufficient stamps on it, given a clear return address on the back of the parcel and sealed the package securely, then you should have no worries. Nor is there any need to hand-deliver your package, unless you really are passing by anyway. You will probably not be able to put it directly into your recipient's hands, and it may become detached from the normal internal mail system. Leave the parcel with the receptionist, ask for a receipt and leave. *Never* cold-call a publisher expecting to be welcomed in for a cup of coffee and a chat.

Two weeks later

If at the end of two weeks you have not yet heard anything from the publisher, it is permissible to write a short, polite follow-up letter, or to make a quick phone call just to check that your package has arrived safely. Your editor may have been away from their desk on holiday, at a sales conference or attending a book fair and has returned to a teetering pile of unsolicited manuscripts all demanding attention. You do not want to sound like you are nagging, or aggrandizing yourself.

Six weeks later

Assuming your initial follow-up letter or phone call proved that your manuscript had arrived, you must then wait a further six weeks before your next follow-up letter. In this case, there is little point in telephoning. Write another polite enquiry about your manuscript. A brief letter sent after an appropriate gap may jog a busy editor's memory. But remember to leave at least six weeks between letters. An editor who feels pressured into making a decision will usually decide to reject.

In fact, we ought to make a particular point of this: if you demand an immediate reaction from an editor, that reaction will very likely be a resounding 'No!'. Think about it. You are an editor with a desk teeming with work, both commissioned and unsolicited, and you are under a lot of pressure. Someone keeps sending you nagging letters asking about their manuscript. What is the quickest way of bringing this to a stop? Send the manuscript back. And what if your editor felt they *almost* liked your book, but were not entirely convinced and wanted to dwell on it for a while, or seek other opinions? Your complaining letters could put a stop to that by putting the editor under more pressure.

It may be that your project really does require that you meet the editor face to face to explain some computer innovation or distinctive new video animation showreel or laptop computer display. In this case, *send* as much information as you can and request an appointment to meet with the editor should they feel your project as explained on paper is one in which they may be interested. Do make sure that you give the editor some idea of what you wish to discuss in advance. It is a waste of everyone's time for you to arrive at a hard-won appointment only to find within the first few seconds that your idea does not fit in with that particular publisher's requirements or list. Do not expect a decision on the spot. Even if the editor with whom you have met is enthusiastic about your project, it is likely these days that any purchasing decision will have to be made by a whole team of different, though interested, parties.

Timing of submissions

The last thing on your mind is likely to be an appropriate time of year for submitting your work. You struggle with it for however many months it takes, you strive to make it look professional, you place it tenderly in an envelope, and you post it off to the appropriate publisher. Nevertheless, it is as well to be aware that there are definite 'black holes' in the year.

Many, many people have a dream that one day their work will be published. Projects and manuscripts are being sent in all the time. Editors are always busy, but some times are busier than others. For instance, the weeks surrounding major national or international book fairs are especially fraught. The main ones are the Bologna Children's Book Fair, the Frankfurt Book Fair and the London Book Fair; and in the USA, the ABA (American Booksellers' Association) Convention.

The summer is also a peak sales conference and holiday period which will take editors away from their desks. Some European publishers and agencies will actually close for two or three weeks completely.

If you do submit material in March/April or September/October, give it a little longer before you decline into stereotypical head-banging movements and deep, continuous moaning.

To be honest, there is not a perfect time to submit your manuscript. By far the best approach is to send it off and fill in the time by getting to work on your next project.

Send off project number one. Start on project number two. Send off project two. Start on project number three. *Get a publisher's response for project number one*. See how it works?

Make a submission index

To be extra efficient, you could make an index using a card, book or computer filing system to keep track of your submissions.

If you use a card index, it could look like this:

(Title) *The Zany Zoo*   (Year) 2001

(Submitted to)

<u>Krazey Books</u>, Anne Eddittorre, 14 January '01. Acknowledged 23 January '01. Reminder letter 1 March '01. Material returned 1 April '01, editor commented: 'It's too crazy for us'.

<u>Alfabetti Publishing</u>, John Mindchanger 2 April '01. Mat. retd. 11 April '01 with comment: 'We've decided to publish only alphabet books'.

You can file your submission details in any way you find practical, in alphabetical or month order, and that way keep track of what is where and when a reminder letter could be reasonably sent. It can also include any information which might be useful. For example, you now know that John Mindchanger is seeking only alphabet books. Could you write one?

If John Mindchanger also moves to another publisher before you have sold *The Zany Zoo*, it will also remind you that he has seen it before. He might want to see it again if he is now commissioning books about zoos, but if *The Zany Zoo* is now a year unsold, he might think 'Hmm, wonder why no one else has bought it?', in which case, send him something else.

Multiple submissions

Impatient? Want to cut corners? Want to cover all the bases? Then write an all-purpose letter headed 'Dear Publisher'. Photocopy this letter and send it off to a whole bunch of publishers at the same time, along with some poorly photocopied pages of your typescript.

No! We are joking!

This would be a really, really rotten idea. Sadly, there is no way of cutting corners in publishing. Publishers like to feel special; they get all huffy and irked if they think you have sent your manuscript or project off to anyone else at the same time. They like to feel *chosen*. Never send a photocopied submission letter. Print or type a fresh one out for each publisher, no matter how time-consuming this may seem.

If you really cannot bear to wait, or if one publisher seems to be taking an unreasonable length of time considering your work, then send your work to no more than three publishers in total. If you do feel the need to do this, then make a careful note of who has what, and when they got it, in your meticulous index system. Trust us, if you are not careful, you could end up in a terrible and potentially embarrassing and damaging muddle.

Copyrighting your work

There is obviously no way of copyrighting *ideas* or concepts (meaning an idea thought or spoken about) but as soon as you commit your idea to *paper*, (or your concept to some tangible form – for example, a sculpture) it is in fact copyrighted. Typing 'copyright' and your name and date, or the copyright symbol, ©, on your work affords no further protection. If you really want to protect the copyright in your work, then by far the simplest way is to post it to yourself! You seal your project in an envelope and take it off to the post office. Ask the staff to date stamp it across the sealed flap, and obtain a receipt or proof of post slip.

When you receive the package back through the mail, *do not open it!* Store it away safely somewhere *unopened*. If you are feeling especially nervous, you could even store it with your bank or with your solicitor, although you will most likely have to pay for this additional security. If you think you have a potentially multimillion dollar idea, and are concerned that it could be it stolen, the additional expense may seem worth it. Should it then ever become necessary to prove that you were the first person to write down this idea, then the unopened and date-stamped envelope should provide sufficient proof when opened, for instance, in court.

Some other things to remember

Before you finally submit your finished work, note the following.

Keeping ideas safe

We shall remind you once again not to go around explaining all your best ideas to people. Get your ideas down onto paper first, and then keep them to yourself. Any other medium (a computer disc, for example) is easily alterable, could become corrupted or wiped, and therefore is not safe. If one of your brilliant ideas suddenly appears elsewhere, you can prove where it originated.

Plagiarism

Stealing other people's copyrighted ideas is called plagiarism. It means you have copied or used another person's work without permission. If you wish to quote other people, or emulate their artistic style, always seek permission first. Otherwise someone, somewhere, someday may knock on you door with a legal action.

Copyright is an involved and specialist branch of law, and becoming more so all the time. There are books available on the subject and experts in the field. If in doubt, *always* seek advice from an expert in the field such as an intellectual property lawyer or copyright consultant.

Libel, doubtful taste and other things

Libel is another subject which we do not have the space to cover extensively. We are in the same situation as you could be when doing historical research: where do you stop? We know of children's books being withdrawn from public bookshelves because they have become the subject of a libel action, never to be seen or discussed again. In this book we have deliberately chosen not to name the authors of our sources to protect the innocent *and* the guilty! The dead cannot sue, but the neighbour whom you hate and include as a rather nasty character in your children's novel may well recognize themselves. They may also have little difficulty proving it to a court. Yes, your characters and situations will probably come from life if they are to be realistic, but use your common   sense   and   imagination   to   mix   them   up   into unrecognizable and untraceable people and events. Have you seen those disclaimers at the end of some fiction television programmes and films? The producers here are trying to protect themselves from anyone claiming to recognize themselves in a character.

You can also create expensive trouble for yourself, in terms of reputation as well as money, if you pretend to be someone or something you are not. Never claim to be a university professor in an attempt to impress a publisher. Nor pretend to be a child prodigy if you are eligible for a pension.

Your publisher will most likely edit out any unsuitable language, situations or view you may personally hold which could upset others. These days book contracts contain extensive libel and other warranty clauses. Check your facts if you are going to be contentious, and be moderate and sensible in other areas, for example, cooking recipes and scientific experiments must include clear safety instructions and guidelines. You do not want to be confined to your home because there is an angry mob and a gang of reporters outside waiting to pounce.

Trademarks

If you come up with a great character or concept (or even in this case a title) which you want to protect more firmly than can be done by copyright, then you may wish to consider having it trademarked. There are specialist trademark agents who will do this for you, at a price, or you can do it yourself – in much the way that it is theoretically possible for you to negotiate your own house sale or purchase, if you have the time, diligence and patience. The best place to start your research into this subject is a reference library, writer's reference book, the business telephone pages or online.

Agents

It may seem to you that to employ an agent as a go-between just adds a pointless layer of bureaucracy to the whole process of getting your work published. This is not actually the case, and you may find that an agent can be an invaluable asset in your attempts to see your work in print.

In the publishing world there are various go-betweens: literary or authors' agents, illustrators' agents, theatrical agents, merchandising agents and so on. These are specialists who know intimately the field in which they work.

Of course, they do not work for free. On average, an authors' agent will take between 10 and 25 per cent of basic commission. An illustrators' agent may take 25 to 50 per cent, and a merchandising agent from 40 to 60 per cent.

'Forget that', you may be thinking, but bear in mind that 80 per cent of *something* is a lot more than 100 per cent of *nothing*. And that may be the choice you are faced with, as many publishers these days do not even *look* at unsolicited work unless it has come to them via an agent. There is a practical reason for this: publishers do not have the time or finances to deal with the costly business of going through heaps of unsolicited material. At least when they agree to look at a manuscript or project recommended to them by an agent, they will know that a stringent grading process has already taken place. In other words, they are not going to be sent unsuitable and unpublishable, half-thought-out ideas. An agent will be too intent on maintaining their reputation to do that.

The problem you may find is that it is really not much easier to have your work taken on by an agent than it is to find an interested publisher. The *big* difference is that an agent may see some spark of talent or originality in your work and be prepared to give you the necessary guidance so that the spark can ignite. Very often a large publishing house will be too busy with its own projects to afford you very much advice if yours is rejected.

If an agent agrees to take on the task of trying to sell a piece of work by you, then you can be sure that the agent is fairly convinced that they will be able to find a home for it. As with publishers, agents cannot afford to waste time and resources trying to sell unplaceable projects or services.

You will be able to find the names of the major players in the world of agents via a writer's reference book, authors' agents associations, word of mouth if you know anyone involved in children's publishing, or by meeting them at book talks, book societies or conferences. Another possible way of choosing an agent could be to write a brief, polite letter to a publisher who handles the kind of work you are producing, and asking them if they could recommend any agents to you. (If you do try this route, remember to supply a stamped, self-addressed reply envelope.)

You should submit your work to an agent in exactly the same way as you would to a publisher, but first of all ensure that the chosen agent is actually in the business of accepting unsolicited manuscripts. Many agents these days have a full client list and are unable to expand that list.

One agent we know was sent an unsolicited typescript whilst she was away on holiday, to her home address. She returned to find the police in attendance, enquiring after her health. The author had summoned them in a panic when he had not received an immediate response.

Some agents require a contribution towards their editorial costs for considering your material, so check on this in advance, as well as requesting a copy of their commission schedule. This will outline their commission percentages and detail any extra charges, say, for emergency delivery or photocopying. An agent will have to invest time, faith and money in you before they see a return for their efforts. Commission will be deducted only from work they sell or act for on your behalf.

An agent who likes your work should want to arrange a meeting with you, if at all feasible. At this meeting you should be able to get a clearer idea of what your agent is like, as well as this being an opportunity for the agent to get a look at you. You will be able to ask questions face to face – possibly for the very first time with a professional – and establish what is expected from both parties.

Remember, this may turn out to be a career-long relationship. Agents tend to stay in one place, unlike many publishing editors. Your agent may well end up as a friend, confidant, editor, accountant, security blanket, a shoulder to cry on and so on. It is as well to consider upfront whether this person is someone you would feel happy working with long term on many different projects.

Also, it is as well to find out what kind of an operation they are running. Is it a one-person show working from home? Are they a well-established company? Do they have a client list of children's authors, or do they mainly represent other areas? Are they right in there with the day-to-day cut and thrust of the publishing world? Will you be asked to sign a contract with the agent? Last, but not least: are you prepared to accept their advice?

From your agent, you can expect editorial advice, representation, legal and contractual negotiations, invoicing and chasing of monies and royalties, mediation, as well as information on work required by publishers which may be suitable for your talents.

Incidentally, 'representation' means that the agent will endeavour to place your work with an appropriate publisher and for a good price. No one would suggest that publishers might try to underpay you for your work, but publishers are first and foremost business people and they are out for a good deal. An agent will know the going rate for your work and will ensure you get it.

An agent will also be able to go over the contract with a fine-tooth comb and wrinkle out any little oddities that may have crept in. It can happen, and you are unlikely to be so well up with the small print in publishers' contracts to spot the odd percentage point shaved off your royalties.

In essence, a good agent needs to be a Jack- or Jill-of-all-trades in the publishing world and should have the knowledge and contacts to be able to step in and help you at every stage of the publishing procedure.

So the question remains: do you need an agent? Well, not if you do not mind becoming an expert in the ever-changing world of publishing and contractual law. Not if you do not need to have a knowledgeable professional in your corner when a publisher is causing you problems. Not if you are happy to keep detailed accounting records and are able to fully comprehend the complexities of royalty statements. In all these areas and more, a good agent should be an enormous asset, and you would be wise to investigate this possibility before deciding to go it alone.

One final word: you will need as much professionalism and persistence to find an agent as you would to find a publisher.

A submission checklist

1. Proposal (synopsis, contents, chapters or complete script, of which you have kept a copy).
2. Folder for proposal.
3. Stamped, self-addressed envelope or return postage label (or voucher if you are submitting something overseas).
4. Stamped, self-addressed acknowledgement card.
5. Submission letter (plus curriculum vitae if you have one, and if it bears relevance to your proposal).
6. Your name and address on everything.
7. Make a note of date submission posted in your index record system.
8. Good luck!

Oh, and don't forget to post the package: as one author said to us,

The most useful piece of advice that anyone gave me was: 1. Finish the book, and 2. It won't get published lying in a drawer somewhere.

10 | DEALING WITH REJECTION

Dear U. Sless-Writer,

I return your pathetic manuscript herewith. It was without doubt the worst pile of incompetent, half-assed, illiterate garbage it has ever been my misfortune to waste two hours of my life by reading.

If you should choose to write another book in the same vein, please hesitate to SEND IT SOMEWHERE ELSE!

Your splenetically,

Penny d'Redful

Editor

All those sequestered hours in your lonely garret. All that work, love, care and attention that you lavished on your project, and some ignorant publisher who would not know a bestseller if it marched up to them in the street wearing an 'I am a best-seller' T-shirt and punched them on the nose, has sent it back! *Arrrrrgh*!

Well, you can rest assured about one thing: you will never get a rejection letter like the one above. Publishers are invariably polite in print, no matter what they may privately think of your work.

In order to get some idea of why your work has been rejected, you really need some basic understanding of the way that the world of publishing actually functions. Of course, a book on 'How To Write' is not going to have space to go into the complexities of the cut-throat world of publishing in detail (in fact this book is over 20,000 words longer than originally anticipated). For an in-depth look at this, we recommend you take a look at *Inside Book Publishing* (3rd edition) by Giles Clark and its companion website, www.insidebookpublishing.com This will give you a broad understanding of the who, what, when, where and why in publishing, as well as furnishing you with an extended bibliography and a lot of useful addresses and links.

So, how come you have been rejected?

Let us briefly follow the progress of your unsolicited manuscript as it passes from the hands of the postal service and enters the hallowed turf of the publisher of your choice.

The task of dealing with your manuscript will very likely fall to a junior editor. Alternatively, your manuscript may be looked at by someone on unpaid work experience, or a freelancer brought in especially to help with a large backlog of work, or even just someone who happens to have a spare five minutes.

Face it, your unsolicited manuscript is not going to be prioritized. It may be read 'in-house' (that is, by someone on the publisher's pay roll), or it may be sent out to an outside 'reader' or possibly two, if you are lucky. This reader will be someone whose opinion is trusted by publishers and who will be given a set fee for their report on your manuscript. They may be a teacher with a known wide experience of books of the sort you have sent in, or a freelance editor or some other well-read person whose views have some weight with the publisher. The idea is that this reader will give as objective an opinion of your work as is possible.

Naturally there really is no such thing as real objectivity when you are addressing something as broad as children's literature. Even when it comes to prizewinners, some people are devoted fans and others would not have the books in the house. Despite this, a good reader should be able to give a fair assessment even if the book you have sent in is a fantasy, and that reader personally hates fantasy!

If your manuscript is to be read by such a person, then you need to bear in mind that it will have to be *sent* to that reader. This obviously adds to the time that you will have to wait before getting a response. And if the reader's report is a little equivocal, then the editor may well seek a second opinion. See how six weeks can easily pass before you hear anything?

The final decision will rest with the commissioning editor who is already under performance pressure, with an increasingly busy schedule in a tough economic climate. Your script could be out of your sight for quite some time, but this need not be cause for despair. Indeed, if your manuscript comes back to you really rather rapidly, attached to what looks like a very standard, impersonal letter, then the chances are that one of the following has happened: your manuscript has not been looked at; your manuscript has only been glanced at; you have chosen the wrong publisher; your material is way off target; or the editor simply hated it and does not want to hurt your feelings!

Such a letter will read:

> Thank you for the submission of your script, but I am afraid it is not suitable for our list.

Or:

> I enjoyed reading your submission and found it rather sweet, however the storyline is not strong enough for our requirements.

If you have submitted a non-fiction work concerned with capital punishment down the centuries, then the use of the word 'sweet' would strongly suggest that the person responding has not actually read your work. And 'strong' is a frequently used word which means whatever the publisher wants it to mean, usually not a lot, to be honest.

Other 'standard' rejection letters include the wording:

> We are not looking for unsolicited scripts at the moment.

Or:

> We are not publishing new authors in the current economic climate.

Your first reaction to such a rejection may be, 'The fools! I'm going to give them a piece of my mind! They need to understand the terrible mistake they have made by rejecting me!'

Seriously, folks: do not bother. If they are not interested at this time, then they are not interested. An irate letter demanding an explanation will only alienate you. Move on!

Perversely, the longer the rejection letter, *coupled* with the length of time it took to reply, the more the publisher liked your work. This may sound a little odd at first, but think about it. If all the publisher can be bothered to do is to write two lines, then that is because they do not feel they have anything helpful to say. If you get two pages of criticism, apparently tearing your work to shreds, that means the editor in question was sufficiently impressed to spend time on not only going through your manuscript in some detail, but also thought it worth while giving you the benefit of their experience and opinion.

For an author this can be a difficult thing to handle, but the more your work is criticized the better it is for you in the long run. One well-known children's author told us the following:

> *I once wrote a TV sitcom and sent it to the BBC. It came back accompanied by the following 'though there's the occasional good line, your dialogue, if literate, is too literary, and often in the form of a paperback novel. Situation comedy means what it says: comedy arising from and furthered by a strong situation. Here we have only endless conversation, mostly with the same subjects under discussion, resulting in some heavy-handed plotting of a feather-weight storyline'.*

Did that author turn to flower arranging classes? No, he goes on to say this:

> *Useful advice? Definitely! I'd been told I could write good lines; that I had the style of a novelist (albeit minor); and that I was literate. My writing ambition switched overnight. There were still plenty of failures to come – but it was a turning point for me.*

Reader's reports

If an editor comments on your work either constructively or critically, you should not assume that the editor has actually read your work. They may well be quoting from a reader's report or two. If the report is constructive, the editor may send you a copy. This can be very helpful; just remember that it was not intended for your eyes and do not take any criticism too harshly. In fact, if your work is non-fiction, it is more than likely that your work will have been read by a third party with some expertise in the field in which you have written.

A reader's report will usually show the editor the length of the work and the market for which it is intended. It will include, in the case of a work of fiction, a brief summary of the plot. It will then detail strengths and weaknesses, outline particular points that need to be addressed by the author and then end with a 'verdict' as to whether, in the reader's opinion, the manuscript would benefit from being rewritten or if it is beyond hope, or if it is just what the publisher has been looking for.

If, in the letter of rejection, the editor comments that they liked your work, albeit not quite enough, and that they would be interested in reading anything else you may write, then you can feel very pleased with yourself. This is a great step forward! It means that for one of several reasons the work you submitted was not quite right for them, but that they were sufficiently impressed by it to wish to consider something else by you.

Could it be that your work is not quite what that publisher is producing right now? Make sure you have a recent catalogue of that publisher's output and take a look at what is in there. Might you be able to come up with something that may suit them better? This publisher is worth following up!

If you receive a helpful and reasonably lengthy rejection letter, some of which you may genuinely not understand, or you believe the editor has completely missed the point, then a brief, professional telephone call to that editor is now permissible. Do not be surprised if you find that the editor has not actually read you script, but tried to save themselves some time because their readers firmly recommended a rejection. Be friendly, and be forgiving. An editor has been known to ask an author to resubmit their material!

Conversely, if you sense a certain dismissive tone between the lines of your brief rejection letter, then it may well be that the editor simply did not like your style or the work you presented. In this case, if you decide to approach the same publisher again with your next offering, it may be wise to write to a different editor. It may be even wiser to choose a different publisher. Editors are only human and it is not beyond possibility that a particular editor may be having a bad day, and has taken a dislike to your work for no really good reason!

Check your returned package

Beware! If you get a rejected manuscript back, make sure you check it thoroughly before sending it off elsewhere. Make sure it is all there. Make sure the pages are in order and all the right way up. Make sure there are not jam fingerprints on it or coffee-cup stains or claret-glass rings. Cat paw-prints are also tremendously common! It is not unknown for editors to scribble uncomplimentary comments on the actual script (very rude and unprofessional, but it does happen), or accidentally leave a damning page of comments amidst the text. The last thing you need is for the next publisher to be privy to the musings of a publisher who has already rejected your work.

If you do encounter scribbles or accidentally enclosed notes, try to steel yourself for the experience. They may be both eye-opening and deeply wounding. You were probably not meant to see them so remember the old adage: eavesdroppers never hear good of themselves. Rejected authors who read the publisher's notes are unlikely to read good of themselves. Try not to take it too much to heart. One agent we know scribbled a note to her editor, following the cold-calling of an overenthusiastic, scary and eccentric author. Her experienced eye glanced over the 200,000-word story for 5-year-olds and she wrote a note intended for her editor: 'This stuff's rubbish, the guy's bonkers, send it back at once for me with a nice thanks-but-no-thanks note.' It would seem that a well-meaning temporary member of staff returned the note too, because a suicidal and somewhat unpleasant reply swiftly ensued from the recipient. Temporary members of staff who do not know the publishing system (and we are not blaming them) can be responsible for some classic mistakes, including returning only half of your material. Double-check your returned package.

The thing to do before you send your script off for a second, third or fourth attempt is to eradicate any sign that anyone else has ever seen it. If this means printing out a new copy or making another photocopy of the whole thing, then so be it.

We promised our editor we would never suggest that when submitting your typescript you should do dastardly things like putting in a couple of pages upside down or back to front. Nor any other little trick like a carefully placed thread, which might indicate to you that the reader never got beyond page 2 of your submission. So in the classic opt-out line of many an amateur story attempt, those last sentences were 'all a dream'.

The problem with these 'dreams', however, is that many experienced editors realize they are being tested and will carefully replace the thread, or assiduously leave chapters out of order or back to front as received!

Another point: it is not always necessary for your manuscript to be read from start to finish. An editor may instinctively know within the first chapter or two that this project is not for them. This may seem unreasonable to you, but remember what we told you in Chapter 5: grab them by the lapels on page 1!

Most experienced editors or agents admit they will have formed an opinion as to whether it is worth reading the whole script by the time they have read the submission or covering letter and the first chapter or two.

Let us say the senior commissioning editor or even the person calling themselves 'the publisher' of your chosen publishing house really likes your work. These days, unless the publishing firm is a very small business indeed, the recommendation of a single person, no matter how highly placed within that firm, is not enough to secure a contract for you.

Your champion will have to present your work at an 'acquisition meeting' and convince a whole number of other people that will include everyone from other editors and sales and marketing people, to art directors and accountants that they should take your work on.

Without a majority vote in favour, then your work will be returned. Or maybe some of the other people at the meeting may decide they need to take a closer look at your work before coming to a final decision at the next meeting. These meetings may take place only once or twice a month, Once again, you can see how time passes while nothing seems to be happening, and why the passage of time is not necessarily a bad sign from your point of view.

Even if the 'acquisition meeting' votes in favour of your work, the editor will then need to go away and do some 'costings'. They will need to decide how much they can afford out of their annual budget for the initial printing, artwork, design, and editing. They will need to decide what grade paper to use and whether to print in hardback first or risk a trade paperback publication with all the additional publicity costs that it will engender in order to get the book on the shelves in enough numbers to warrant a large print run. They will need to decide whether illustrations are required and, if so, who should be hired to do them and how much money they will demand for their work. They will need to take a look at their long-term publishing plans and find a suitable publishing date, invariably in the following year!

Even if you get a letter telling you your work was loved and cherished by the acquisition team, you could still be kept on tenterhooks for some weeks while all this unseen work goes on. Your formal acceptance letter could take weeks and weeks to arrive.

We shall stop there, because this chapter is not about what happens when your manuscript/project is accepted. This chapter is about coping with rejections, so let us carry on coping. The authors we consulted said the following:

Don't take any notice of anyone. Just write.

A degree does not mean one is automatically a writer. I had to do my apprenticeship, just like anyone else. It took me seven years to produce a saleable book.

<u>*Don't give up*</u> *if you have* any *signs of real encouragement from publishers. But if every returned manuscript is accompanied by a rejection slip, or a bland and vague letter, take a long hard look at your submissions.*

Keep at it! Writing is a craft as well as an art and needs to be practised assiduously if you want to get published.

Write, write, and re-write, however long it takes. Keep working at it until you make it.

Nothing is ever wasted, because it helps build writing technique.

When is it time to rethink?

The time to rethink the material you are submitting is if you have received, say, three brief and impersonal letters of rejection. In reality, you must begin to assume that the work is somewhat wide of the mark. Perhaps you would be better off trying something new, writing for a different age group or maybe approaching your chosen topic (should you still have faith in it) from a different angle or in a fresh way.

What, though, if you have three longer rejection letters from publishers. What if it is clear from the contents of these letters that people have actually read your work reasonably carefully. And what if the comments you are getting back seem to have some common theme? This is the time for you to give serious thought to the criticisms you have received.

It is a serious waste of your time if you do not take on board the opinions of professionals. Certainly editors can and do make errors of judgement, but on the whole they do have a pretty clear idea of what is going on in the market and whether your work, be it ever so well written, is going to actually sell.

Be aware that tastes and fashions change. You may have written a book that would have sold instantly 20 years ago, but no matter how brilliantly it is written, anything that comes across as dated or old-fashioned will be unlikely to find a home. A book written a year ago may no longer be fashionable, or topical. *All* the authors we spoke to said, 'Study the market'. *All* the authors said, 'Keep at it, keep on writing.' *All* the authors said, 'Revise and rewrite until you succeed'.

Assuming that three publishers have now seen your work and have made similar critical comments, the last thing you should do is to carry on stubbornly sending the unaltered manuscript/project off in the hope that someone will have a better opinion of it. By doing this, all you will effect is to 'spoil' the market for your work. Three publishers have seen it and rejected it. You need to *revise your work* before submitting it again.

Unless one of the rejecting publishers has actually *asked* you to revise and re-submit, it is not worthwhile sending them a rewritten version. Send it to someone new and see what they say.

It is almost like engaging in a treasure hunt. The prize is publication, and along the way you will pick up various clues which allow you to move on to the next step. Simplistically, one publisher may tell you your work is far too long. You shorten it. The next publisher may tell you the language is inappropriate for the target age group. You amend accordingly. The next publisher may point out redundant characters and confusions in the plot line. You attend to them. Do you see what is going on? By taking on board these constructive criticisms, you are honing your work for the market.

If you have patience, some talent and the ability to take criticism on board and learn by it, then you are well on the way to getting your name in print.

In the past, it was possible that an editor who perceived some worthwhile spark in a rejected work, would have the time to nurture you along until you produced a polished and consummate manuscript. Sadly, that is seldom the case these days. Increasingly publishers seem to be demanding material of such high quality and presentation that it could almost be sent straight to the printers without the publisher even having to touch it!

If you find it hard to make coherent sense of all the criticisms of your rejected work, then maybe this is the time to present it to one of the criticism services we mentioned earlier. Or if you are in a writers' group, maybe you should take it along for general appraisal (if you are not in a writers' group or class, this may be the time to seek one out).

Just remember that the nearer you get to possible publication, the more the criticism will be stepped up as editors start fine-tuning and adjusting your work for the marketplace.

This may be the time to approach an agent. If you have several near-miss rejection letters from different publishers, these may help to gain an agent's attention, bearing in mind that an agent will usually be better able to give you long-term advice and encouragement than will a publisher. Therefore, send these letters off with your manuscript: agents understand only too well how hard it is for a new author to get a foot in the publishing door and can read between the lines of an editor's rejection letter. They are familiar with the good old catch-22 situation: 'Come back when you've made a name for yourself and we'll publish your stuff'.

One author we know had a spoof middle-fiction novel submitted to a publisher via an agent. The story revolves around a girl who wants to be a secretary when she leaves school, marry a hunky super-hero and live happily ever after. Her mum, who is a boot-wearing, Green feminist building labourer, has other ideas, and her step-dad is no help in his house-management role. The first publisher who saw the script rejected it along with a two-page letter of disgust to the agent. That publisher missed the point: they took the plot seriously. The second publisher telephoned to say that he thought he ought to buy the story but had been unable to read it himself, and no work was being done in his department. His staff had hijacked the script and all he could hear were peals of laughter!

When you do, sooner or later, find someone who likes your style, or your humour, or your imagination, what happens next is only the beginning! Read on.

11 | DEALING WITH ACCEPTANCE

(Brring-brring. Brring-brring)

Hello?

Hello, there. Could I speak to Miss Hope ffulle-Author, please?

Speaking.

Hi! It's Anne Eddittorre, here. I have some wonderful news for you! I took your book to our acquisitions meeting this morning, and I'm thrilled to be able to tell you that everyone totally loved your work and we really want to publish it!

(Thud of Hope hitting the floor unconscious)

It will happen something like that. A telephone call out of the blue to tell you that all your hopes, desires and dreams have finally come true. Of course, it is not obligatory for you to collapse into a theatrical swoon on the carpet. But you are allowed to celebrate in one or more of the following ways: run around the room, screaming; run down the street, screaming; call all your friends and family and scream at them; just stand there clutching the phone and scream.

Once the ear-shattering cadences of your screams have faded there are several things you need to do.

First, and this is the really down-to-earth and gloomy bit, you must keep in the back of your mind the adage: there is many a slip 'twixt cup and lip. In other words, a telephone call telling you that your work has been accepted is a long way from the day when the finished book will triumphantly land on your doormat, not to mention quite a distance from an *official* offer on paper. You can (and should) express your profound delight to Anne Eddittorre, but you must also tell her that you are looking forward to receiving the offer *in writing*. Just supposing Anne went sick from work for six months, or was 'rationalized' and changed jobs the day following her call, or some other disaster occurred? We are not trying to unduly alarm you, but what proof have you at this stage that Anne made an offer to buy your book?

At its simplest, a letter with your offer will probably look something like this:

Dear Hope,

I am delighted to be able to make you an offer for MY FIRST CHILDREN'S BOOK which we propose publishing in our My First Book series in the Spring of 2002. We all think this is a wonderfully imaginative and well crafted story.

I can offer an advance of ££$$ payable as to half on signature of the contract and half on first publication against royalties of X per cent of the published price on paperback copies sold in the home market, and X per cent on copies sold for export. We require World Volume rights.

I do hope this offer is acceptable and look forward to hearing from you. I will have the contract drawn up as soon as possible.

With best wishes

Anne Eddittorre
Senior Commissioning Editor

Ignoring any typing and spelling mistakes, and any complicated inclusions for a moment, the great majority of children's publishers behave in an honest and honourable fashion, and when they make you an offer, it will most likely result in your work being published. (But cancellations *do* happen for a variety of reasons, and it would be unfair of us to pretend otherwise.)

The advance

What exactly is an 'advance'? Let us say your publisher offers you an advance of £1,000. The actual offer may say something like: 'an advance of £1,000 set against a royalty of 10 per cent of the published price of the hardback edition for Home Sales'. (Home sales means sales in the domestic market; foreign sales, or export sales, means sales of the book in other countries.)

This £1,000 is the amount of money you will be paid in advance of any actual sales of copies of the book itself. You will be asked to sign a contract (more of that in a moment). The advance may come to you as, say, £500 when both you and the publisher have signed the contract, and a further £500 upon publication of the book itself. This money is paid in acknowledgement of the work you have already done in producing the book. So long as you fulfil your part in the deal set out in the contract, this money is non-returnable.

Published price and royalties

The published price referred to in the offer is the recommended retail price. Say your book sells for £5 at 'home'. For every copy of your book sold at £5, you will be entitled to a 'royalty' of 10 per cent, in this case, 50p. *However*, the £1,000 advance you receive is an advance 'set against a royalty of 10 per cent'. That means you will not see any more money until enough 50ps have accumulated to cover the £1,000 advance. Which therefore means, in this case, that 2,000 copies of your book have to be sold before you will see any royalty money.

Unfortunately, the above scenario is a lot less complicated than the real thing. Anyway, you have received the publisher's offer and having read the rest of this chapter carefully, let us say you are happy with the offer. You must then reply in writing to your editor, accepting the offer, and the basic wording should include the following:

Dear Anne,

Re: MY FIRST CHILDREN'S BOOK

Thank you for your letter dated XXXX regarding your offer to publish the above title in your My First Book series. I am pleased to accept the offer as outlined, subject to contract.

I look forward to receiving and considering the contract in due course, and to working with you.

With all good wishes,

Hope ffulle-Author

Obviously every book and every offer letter is different, and you will be replying accordingly, but the important basic wording you need to include is 'I accept the offer as outlined' and 'subject to contract'. This will give you an opportunity to examine the contract and perhaps negotiate some changes before you commit yourself. The same thing applies at this stage if you are being offered a 'flat-fee' payment (a flat fee is a single payment without royalties). In this case, the offer letter from the publisher may include wording along the following lines:

> We would be delighted to include your text piece on FOUR COLOUR PRINTING in our Encyclopedia of Publishing.
>
> We will pay a flat fee of £$£ for your 800-word contribution upon delivery and acceptance of the text, for exclusive rights in all languages, all forms, editions, versions and adaptations throughout the world, and an acknowledgement will be given to you in the front of the book. We aim to publish in October 2003, and will give to you one copy of the title upon publication.
>
> Please sign the attached copy of this letter where indicated as acceptance of our terms.

In this case, the payment for your contribution is *all* the money you will receive. Because the publisher wants exclusive rights throughout the world, they can sell as many copies as they like, in whatever form, and you cannot sell that piece of text anywhere else. If you are happy with this, sign and date the copy letter and return it to the publisher.

Editorial enthusiasm

Suppose the editor informs you that although everyone is very enthusiastic about your book, they would like you to do some revisions under editorial supervision before they are prepared to make you an offer. Anne Eddittorre's letter might say:

> We all really loved your story about the little girls who didn't get any birthday presents, but we all thought it would work a whole lot better if she DID get the presents. And does the main character have to be a little girl? We all felt that a little boy would work much better. What do you think?

You may well think, 'No way!', as this level of 'revision' will change your story almost beyond recognition. You are perfectly entitled to respond in that way, particularly if you think the whole point of your story is about to vanish in a puff of editorial smoke.

However, you will probably find the editorial suggestions are much less drastic than those outlined above, and it surely would not do any harm for you to at least look at them? If it looks like the editor has gone insane over your script with a red pen, when you get to see it at a subsequent meeting, then you can still up sticks and leave with your authorial integrity intact.

Think long and hard before you choose this line of action. You will have your integrity – but who is going to benefit from that? Certainly not all the children who would have enjoyed your book had it been published. Be tough, be realistic. You want to be published: perhaps a certain amount of flexibility at this stage will prove to be of immense benefit in the long run.

Naturally you do not want to be published at any cost, but a degree of give and take and some carefully considered negotiations with your prospective editor may result in a compromise that will suit everyone. Do not be afraid to fight your corner, but beware of being too antagonistic. After all, at this stage in your career an interested publisher is worth more than none at all.

Revising your work

Let us assume you agree to take your manuscript away and do some revising. The editor will probably give you a letter containing their comments and suggestions. They may attach stick-it notes to relevant pages or even make pencilled suggestions in the large margins you have deliberately left for this purpose. Be sure that you understand precisely what is required of you. Sort out any ambiguities in advance. If there are comments which seem a little vague, then pin the editor down and ask *exactly* what they mean. A vague editorial comment is a sign of busyness or laziness: make sure they do their job and thus make your job of revising as painless as possible.

Rewrite and resubmit

Rewriting and resubmitting your work may not be the end of the road. It may well be that your editor is *quite* pleased with the results of your work, but that the book still is not *exactly* what they want. Are you prepared to take yet another look at it with yet another bunch of editorial comments? Their position may well be that they want to ensure that your book is as perfect as possible, bearing in mind that you are a new and unknown author. And it may well be that the book still has flaws in its construction. Try to keep an open mind about this: the editor may be starting to irritate you, but their job is to get as saleable a commodity into the marketplace as they possibly can, which is what you want too.

Development money

Before you re-revise any further, it would not be unreasonable of you to ask for some 'development' money. This is a payment which you get to keep should the publisher finally decide that after all your time and effort, your work is still not going to be accepted. If the publisher does finally accept your work after two or three reworkings, then that money will be deducted (or offset) from the advance or flat-fee offer they then make.

There is no guarantee that your editor will agree to your request, but if you are going to put in a lot of work, plus have your hopes raised, and the end result could be that the publishers still reject, then you are entitled to try for some sort of compensation.

Once everything is in writing and the editor is happy with your revised book, you will get a 'contract'. If you are working through an agent, they will be able to sort out all the fine print and do all the negotiations on your behalf, but it is still useful for you to understand a little of what goes on behind the scenes.

The contract

Basically, when you are sent the official offer letter, the editor will then arrange for an appropriate contract to be sent to you. Depending on the publisher, the contract may be negotiated and drawn up by the editor, a contracts department or a freelance contracts consultant. You could wait some time before receiving the legal documentation. Progress could also be delayed by the type of contract the publisher uses. It could be a simple, single-page document or it could be an incredibly complicated, closely typed, 30-page wadge of paper, in which your book is called a 'media neutral format product'. Those unfamiliar with legal terminology will rapidly find themselves confused.

Never sign anything you do not understand

If you do not understand legal jargon then we strongly suggest that you seek advice before accepting an offer, or signing a contract or contractual letter. The benefit of having an agent at this point, is that part of the agent's job is to understand the small print and to ensure there are no sneaky little clauses very much to the benefit of the publisher at your expense. It happens!

There are books available on contracts and copyright, and information in writer's reference books and on the Web, but unless you feel able to absorb this kind of information at speed, keep up to date on legal developments and become an expert, then you must seek the advice of published authors, authors' societies, writers' advice centres or groups. Best of all is to consult a book publishing and media contracts and copyright expert. It will prove good value to pay for advice now, rather than take any risks. Your family solicitor, incidentally, experienced as they will be in their own fields, may not understand the peculiarities of a publisher's contract, nor are they likely to know whether the terms you are being offered are fair even if they can unravel the jargon.

It is not easy for an inexperienced person to negotiate points in their first contract. You may even be so excited and thrilled at the prospect of getting into print that you will sign anything. Think carefully before you do this! What of the future? There may be a clause in the contract allowing the publisher 'first refusal' of your next work. ('First refusal' means they must be allowed to see your next work and consider whether to publish it before anyone else can see it.) What if you decide you never want to work with them again, and yet are legally bound to offer them your next work? The publisher may hang on to your next work for weeks, or make you a derisory offer, or they may even be a totally unsuitable publishing house for this second work. All these things need to be taken into consideration.

Your offer from the publisher could be a flat-fee payment to use your short story exclusively in an anthology for a specified period of time. The offer may be non-exclusive, which means you can sell the story again, say, to a magazine, even while it is still available in the anthology. The offer could be for an advance giving the publisher the right to sell your book in the one language throughout the world, or it may be for all languages and all media throughout the world, beyond the world, and in perpetuity! And you may be entitled to a share of additional sales made from translation of your work into another language, audio versions, television and so on. Or you may not, and even then the proportions may not be as generous as they should be! If you do not know what is a fair and reasonable offer or contract, if you do not understand what every clause actually means, then you cannot be expected to make a good judgement.

We asked some contracts and copyright experts (including publishers, consultants and society advisers) for their comments:

The trouble with most authors is that they don't ask any questions about contracts. The usual remark is along the lines of 'It looked so official I assumed it must be okay'. Alternatively, they consult their own solicitor who has never seen an author contract before and who asks a mass of niggling little questions. Some authors then try to change the basic terms of a contract once it arrives 'Yes I know I agreed to a 7 per cent royalty but I've heard that 10 per cent is more normal'. Please point out that such things should be agreed before contract stage.

No one ever asks me anything, except what 'special editions' means.

Children's authors often ask me why their royalties tend to be lower than those for other trade books. They also get confused over collaboration with illustrators, and the implications of electronic rights.

A contract is a legally binding document. Even if a publisher says 'This is our standard contract' or the contract is (or appears to be) printed, contracts are negotiable. If in any doubt, consult a specialist. That almost certainly does not include your local solicitor.

Most authors will confess to never actually reading their contracts properly, if at all, when pressed!

We also asked these same experts if they could recount any interesting experiences negotiating contracts. Here are some of the more unusual:

The blind author whose contract expected him to read and correct proofs.

The Australian author who was expected to return corrected proofs to the UK publisher within seven days of their dispatch to the author.

The commissioned illustrator whose contract obliged her to deliver her material two weeks prior to the date of the contract (thus putting her in breach as soon as she signed it).

The agent whose contract provided for the advance to be on account of 'the aforementioned royalties' but the royalty clause came after *the advance clause (the page was reprinted before the contract went off!).*

The publisher's contract commissioning an author to write a work which contained a clause stating that the contract was null and void if the author had not delivered the typescript prior to signing.

Money!

'When can I expect to see some money?' you might well ask. Let us go back in time to when your editor first sends you the offer. You now understand and have agreed the terms in the contract; you have signed and returned the contract. You are camped out by your letterbox waiting for your first cheque to arrive. (The holding of breath is not advised at this point.) You may be required to supply an invoice along with your contract, or if you are being paid a flat fee. Your invoice should contain similar information to the following:

INVOICE no. 111

Date

To: Anne Eddittorre   From: (your name and address)
Senior Commissioning Editor
(address)

Payment due on delivery and
acceptance of short story
entitled I NEED MONEY by
Ian M. Poverished   £1,000

Total: £1,000
PAYMENT ON RECEIPT OF INVOICE

If you are registered for value added tax, or need to include any other information, then do so at the bottom of the invoice.

It could take six weeks for the publisher's accounts department to actually get around to sending you the cheque for the money due on signature of the contract. Various people within a publishing house may have to authorize a payment before it can be made. If you are working with an agent, then add a week or two on to this time, as your cheque will be sent to the agent first in order that they can check the details, clear the cheque, note their records system, and subtract their commission before you get the balance.

Believe it or not, from the time when you are first told that the publishers are interested in your work to the day when the advance cheque arrives could be several months. If revisions are needed or contract negotiations are lengthy, an unbelievable couple of *years* could go by! No, this is not the way to make a fortune, by any stretch of the imagination.

And things do not speed up too much once you have earned out your advance payment. Publishers tend to make up their accounts every six months. Some even do it annually, particularly publishers of foreign editions. This means that the 50p coming to you for a book bought by a child in a store in January, may not actually get to you until, say, October of the same year, if the accounts are made up half-yearly, or, possibly, March of the *following* year for an annual accounts system.

Royalty statements

Royalty statements are documents which will detail how your book is selling, and will show any other sales agreement payments the publisher has made. They will show a date from which the accounts are being calculated, but you may not actually receive the statement for up to four months *after* this date. This statement will include things like home sales and export sales, sales at a greater discount (to book clubs, perhaps), any other income from rights sales made by the publisher (for example, large print rights), and possibly any deductions for copies you may have ordered for your own use. If you do not have an agent to check these statements for you, then you will have to do some careful checking yourself to ensure that you have received all the monies you are entitled to, and that they are the correct percentage shares.

For the most part, these statements of accounts will be honest and accurate, and any errors are genuine mistakes. If you have any doubts, your contract may entitle you, or someone on your behalf, to examine the publisher's books. If you have any other worries, including payment delays, an author's society may be able to advise you how next to proceed.

Rights

There are a variety of other ways in which you and the publisher can earn money from your book, and these include the selling of rights as we have previously mentioned. These are just some of the potential sales areas and rights which could ensue from that first hardback edition of your work:

- hardback, trade paperback, mass-market paperback editions
- anthology rights
- first serial rights (for newspapers or magazines)
- translation rights
- large print (books for those with impaired vision)
- audio (single voice readings, or dramatized readings)
- radio, television, film, video and so on for dramatization
- animation
- merchandising (everything from greetings cards to curtains)
- electronic (CD-ROM, online, e-book and so on).

If you do not have an agent to sell these rights for you, or if you do not have a clue how you would go about selling them for yourself, then the best people to try and sell them are your publishers. If you have any helpful suggestions or contacts, the rights people would be glad to hear of them.

Working with an editor

You will be working closely with an editor. This may not be the person you have been corresponding with thus far. (That person may well be the senior commissioning editor.) Once your work has been accepted for publication, you may find yourself liaising with an editor a little lower down the hierarchical tree.

You will be involved now in revising your work under this editor's guidance, or perhaps just doing a little polishing here and there. Your editor (let us call him/her 'Eddie' for convenience) may also be looking for an illustrator.

Illustrations

If your work is going to be very highly illustrated, you are likely to be sharing your royalties with this illustrator, usually on a basis of around 40 per cent for you and 60 per cent for the artist, depending upon the nature of the work, and sometimes the fame of the artist. (If you are sharing royalties, the chances are that your contract is going to look even more complicated!)

Some publishers will ask for your approval of a chosen illustrator, while others will assume they know best. The level of your veto should be outlined in the contract – if you have any veto at all!

Eddie may invite your comments on the work of several artists while a final decision is being made. You and Eddie will then be able to discuss which artist seems most suitable, but when it comes to the bottom line, unless you have an absolute contractual veto (unlikely!) Eddie has a loaded Kalashnikov machine gun and you are armed with an unloaded banana.

Once an illustrator has been chosen, the first thing you are likely to see are 'roughs' – sketches of the salient points in the book which it has been decided will benefit from illustration.

Book jackets

Your approval will probably be sought for the cover artwork and design. This is an area where the publisher will believe they know best and, with their experience and the input from their sales teams, they probably do. Your job will be to double-check that all the details of the artwork, design, cover 'blurb' and any biographical details are correct. (The 'blurb' is the text mainly seen on the back of a book which tries to sell the contents to the prospective purchaser.)

Proofs

You may possibly not see anything until the 'proofs' turn up. Proofs are, or are like, photocopies of how the book will look with the final layout and all the illustrations in place. If you spot that your heroine has somehow metamorphosed into a giraffe, this is definitely the time to mention it.

The proofs will come with an accompanying letter asking for your comments and giving you a specific period of time in which to respond. It is important that you get your comments in before this deadline, or your silence could be interpreted as approval and the publishing process may continue without your comments being heard. Your editor will tell you how to correct the proofs, especially for when you spot any typographical errors.

By proof stage, the production costs are starting to become expensive, and your contract will probably stipulate that you are unable to make alterations in the text above (usually) 10 per cent, due to the prohibitive cost involved in such changes (unless you are prepared to foot the bill yourself). This is to stop you going into a panic that the whole book is totally wrong and needs thoroughly reworking now you have had a few more months to think about it.

Edited scripts

You may receive a copy of your manuscript edited by a copy-editor and marked up for the typesetter. The chances are that this is going to look like something out of your worst nightmare. Do not panic! The chances are that the majority of the mess covering your script consists of instructions to the typesetter for the removal of typing errors and unwanted indentations.

Some of the scribbles may be grammatical corrections or minor improvements in the flow of the text. If some of the editorial changes go beyond simply tidying the text or making copy-editing alterations, you may find yourself having objections. Take a deep breath, go for a walk or leave the script overnight before you write to Eddie or call him to see if some compromise can be reached. It may be that there is simply a difference of opinion between you and Eddie that can be talked through to mutual satisfaction.

On the other hand, if Eddie has spotted something in your text that is likely to cause offence to a large portion of the potential readership, then you would be well advised to take Eddie's advice and change the offending section rather than risk adversely affecting future sales. If it is practicable, you may well be invited to meet with Eddie (possibly not if you live in Vanuatu and Eddie works in Vancouver) and you may be introduced to other members of the production team. If you get on well with Eddie, you may find yourself in frequent contact with him as he fills you in on progress.

Authors are a curious, self-contained breed, most of whose work is done in solitary confinement, and to suddenly find their book in the hands of an outsider can be a traumatic experience. It will not endear you to the very busy Eddie if you are constantly ringing him up to check on how things are going. Think before you ring. Remember that Eddie will be dealing with several authors at once. Imagine what it must do to your efficiency to have several people calling you up for a chat every day of the week.

If you do have a problem or query and Eddie seems always to be in meetings when you call, then write, fax or e-mail if you really do require a response. You may need to be patient and to learn to cope with what seem to you to be breathtakingly unbusinesslike practices in the world of children's publishing.

What to do if something goes wrong

If something to do with your book has gone wrong and you have enough confidence, then speak to the individual concerned. If the problem is particularly emotive, or if you are unable to reach a compromise verbally, then write to or fax the publisher so that your concerns are made perfectly clear.

If the reaction to this is not satisfactory, then write to the Managing Director and send a copy of your letter to the person with whom you are having the disagreement.

Be firm in your letter, but also try to be as fair and as objective as possible. Make sure the point you are pursuing is of direct relevance to your book, and not simply the product of a clash of personalities or some misunderstanding that has blown up out of all proportion. If even this level of complaint does not bring things to a satisfactory conclusion, then you should seek help according to your needs.

This help may come in the form of an authors' or illustrators' society, an advice centre, a book-trade periodical, a media contracts expert, an agent or even a solicitor with the relevant experience in the publishing world. This advice could end up costing you money, so be sure the point you are arguing is worth it.

Just remember that publishers have a large investment in keeping their authors happy. After all, they are spending a lot of money to get that first book of yours off the launch pad, and hopefully providing the initial impetus for what could be a glittering career. If you and your publisher get on well, this first encounter could be the start of a mutually rewarding, lifelong involvement.

12 PUBLICATION DAY: WHAT NEXT?

So, you have climbed Mount Everest, you have walked on the moon, you have won an Olympic Gold medal and your first book has a publication date. What do you do now?

Go into tax exile? Probably not. Write another book? Well, you should already have done that. Try to get another book published?

Getting to publication day means you have already jumped two of the Big Three hurdles:

1 Getting a publisher to read your first work;
2 Getting a publisher to publish your first work.
3 Getting a second (and third and fourth and ...) piece of work published.

There is no need to become depressed, but it is said that getting your second book published is more difficult than your first. It does happen that some authors throw so much into their first work that they have nothing left for any subsequent projects. This is understandable. You want to present the best to a potential publisher; you may have spent years polishing and honing your first book. A publisher may ask, 'What else do you have to offer?' Panic! What *else*? The publisher needs another book. You write something quickly. The publisher rejects it, saying it is not as good as the first one. Of course it is not! You spent two years over the first one; you rushed this out 'on demand' in six weeks! Welcome to the world of the published author!

Publication

Back to the day-to-day practicalities for a moment. You have seen and corrected the proofs. You have been given a publication date.

The title of your book will probably have appeared, along with a picture of the cover, in your publisher's sales catalogue some six months in advance of this date. The date will have been carefully chosen by your publisher to maximize its sales potential: a wintry tale might come out in October to attract Christmas sales. There are also peak seasonal publication periods – spring and autumn – and traditional publishing days (these were Thursdays, often in the middle of the month, for review and accounting reasons). Publishers are now far more flexible about choosing dates.

Advance copies

A finished copy of your book will usually be sent to you about six weeks in advance of the actual publication date. Thus it is called an 'advance' copy.

Check it thoroughly, but keep calm if you find that things are not absolutely perfect. You may find some 'minor' errors: misspellings in the blurb, or your biography may even be missing. These things may seem like major nightmares to you, but a publisher is unlikely to recall all the books and start again to correct that sort of mistake or omission, because of the expense. Such 'minor' problems will probably not be corrected until a second print run. (There will not be a second print run until all copies of the *first* print run have sold out.) *However*, if you spot that the book jacket has been attached upside down, that pages of the text are missing or out of order, or your name has been misspelt, then these books will definitely need to be reprinted. Call the publisher immediately in case no one else has noticed.

These faults *do* happen although, thankfully, not very often. And it may well be that the author, who is usually the last person to see the finished article, is the first to spot the problem. One agent said this:

> *I have seen book jackets upside down, names spelt correctly on the front cover, and incorrectly on the spine. But I once got a call from an author to say 'Thank you for my advance copy, but the last page containing the climax of my story is missing!'. Three thousand copies were promptly reprinted, at the printer's expense!*

Gratis copies

Your contract will stipulate how many copies of your book you are entitled to receive free upon publication day. *Always* keep at least one copy of every title and edition of your work in a safe place for the future. If you have given all your copies away, it may be difficult to track down your books if they are no longer on sale in ten years' time. You will also be entitled to purchase further copies at probably the lowest trade discount a publisher would offer to a retailer. (Note, though, you are not supposed to sell these copies and keep the profit yourself, unless you are a bookseller! Check with your publisher if you need copies to sell at, say, a school author visit.)

Lead titles

In the publishing world, a 'lead title' is one which is going to be promoted in preference to all other titles being produced by the publisher. It seldom happens that the first work by an unknown author is going to get this sort of attention. We know of one new author whose first 32-page picture book was published at the same time as a biography of a very famous person which captured world media attention for weeks. He could not understand why his title was not receiving the same attention!

You need to get things into perspective. To you, the publication of your first book may be the climax of a lifetime of ambition, but to the publisher it is just another book on their list, another cog in the machine, another piece of the corporate jigsaw. To the wholesale buyers, it is one more title amongst the thousands published in a year.

Sales and publicity

By publication day, you should have been sent a publicity questionnaire. If you are under the wing of a large publisher, you may already have spoken to someone in the publicity department to discuss ways in which your book can be promoted.

It is one of the unfortunate aspects of the general tendency towards cutting costs to the bone that the publicity departments are often the first to suffer. This cost-cutting is particularly noticeable in the publicity departments that deal with children's books: some publishers will employ freelance publicists for special titles or a new series of titles.

Your publisher's sales team, both directly employed and freelance, will also have been busy attending sales conferences and pre-selling titles (including yours) to bookshops, wholesalers, library buyers and so on. They will have been provided with advance information sheets to distribute, sometimes 9 months in advance of publication day! Hundreds or thousands of copies may be pre-sold or subscribed (known as 'subbed') prior to the big day. You should know, however, that these copies are not definite sales until the copies pass from the retailer into the hands of a paying customer.

Returns

Retailers sometimes return unsold copies of books to the publisher, which will show up as negative amounts on your royalty statement. Publishers will bear this possibility in mind and will 'hold back' a certain amount of royalty money to cover this likelihood. It is known as a 'reserve against returns', and the exact details will be found in your contract.

Reviews

As well as getting your book into the stores, your publisher will also be sending out copies to appropriate people for 'review' purposes. One of the best things you can hope for upon publication of your book is that it gets a glowing review in a magazine, newspaper, online bookseller or children's book website read by potential purchasers, particularly booksellers, teachers and librarians. It is said that no publicity is bad publicity, and any review will draw attention to your title.

A critical review, although depressing, is in the vast majority of cases only a matter of one person's opinion. Your book must have had *something* about it to have attracted the reviewer's attention in the first place.

You cannot please everyone all of the time, and the fact that your book is now in the public domain and in a position to be criticized is proof that a good many people have faith in your work.

(You should know that sending out copies for review is an expensive business for your publisher, and you will not receive royalties for books given away for publicity purposes.)

Most publishers will subscribe to a 'cuttings' service, provided by a firm specializing in scouring all printed material for reviews, comments or whatever of books published by a particular organization. All such pieces of printed publicity are then sent to the publisher in question, who will then send copies of all these cuttings to you. They may range from coverage in a local paper to mentions in national newspapers and magazines. The problem is that you will be sent the reviews whether they are good or bad. A cuttings service is a cost-effective way for your publisher to know who is saying what about your book.

Keep a publicity file. Good reviews and publicity can later be put to good use, perhaps when approaching a different publisher further along your career trajectory.

The space available for reviewing children's books is notoriously limited, and it would not be wildly unusual for you not to see any reviews of your book at all, good, bad or indifferent. This is not the end of the world, though, regarding children's books. Children's books, particularly the 12+ titles, have become bestsellers through word of mouth. Children make excellent critics, and if they like something, a book can become a must-have, must-read item. Children also like to collect: thus, if they like one title in a series, they are quite likely to buy and read the entire range.

Most of the efforts that publishers seem to make in the world of publicity (television, radio, poster advertising and so on) are confined to adult 'blockbuster' type books. It may seem a curious fact that publishers appear to spend a whole pile of money on books that look set to become bestsellers *anyway*, while not giving any noticeable 'push' to the books that might actually benefit from some publicity. This is one of those quirks of marketing that is all bound up with finances and budgets, and means that large-scale publicity does not often occur for a new book by a new author.

Prizes and awards

Many prizes and awards are granted each year to children's books. Your publisher will be aware of these, and will know the appropriate time to make submissions. You could ask your editor, or publicist if you have one, where they are sending copies of your books for reviewing purposes and whether there are any suitable prizes for which your book can be entered. Depending on timing, any such prize could be awarded in the year, or even two years, after the publication of your book. In any event the press attention and publicity surrounding the presentation of an award is guaranteed to increase sales.

Self-publicity and promotion

Does your book have some topical angle which could attract publicity? Is there a 'hook' upon which to hang some PR (public relations: another way of saying publicity)? Is there something in or from your life that will make the publication of your book of particular interest to the media? Does your book connect with some anniversary, event or topical issue? Most books, whether fiction or non-fiction, contain something in them which can be used to advantage. Something may happen by coincidence in the news to which you can link your book for some useful publicity.

Speak to your publisher's publicity department and see what ideas they can suggest. If you find that your publisher does not have the time or the budget to do all that they might, then have a go yourself. Local newspapers are often very willing to write about a local celebrity ('Local Person Makes Good!') and their first book, and may even publish a photograph into the bargain. Local radio stations may also be interested, particularly if there is an extra newsworthy angle. If your publicist is unwilling or unable to produce a press release or information sheet on your book, then consider writing or designing one yourself.

Visit your local bookstore or make an appointment to meet with the person who runs it. Suggest that you would be willing to visit the store and sign books for customers. If it is a story or poetry book, you could also read from it. Many local booksellers would be only too happy to accommodate you, and would be glad of the local press publicity such an event would be likely to promote. You may have to make personal arrangements if you want a photograph taken, and in some cases, you may even be asked to do the write-up (the article) yourself for the local newspaper if a reporter cannot attend.

Such signing sessions need not be limited to bookshops, either. You could also generate some publicity for yourself by signing copies of your book at a school fair, a garden centre, supermarket or boat/ferry trip; anywhere, in fact, where books are being sold.

Signing sessions can have varying rates of success for no readily apparent reason. You could sell out copies of your book in half an hour, or find that a huge local media blitz only results in half a dozen sales in an entire day. Still, what have you got to lose? It all means more sales, more publicity and eventually, more money.

Your library may also be interested in a visit from a local author if you are prepared to read your story book to a group of children at a story-telling session. Contact the children's librarian for your area.

Visit online booksellers and complete or update the 'About the author', comments and reviews section associated with your publication.

Visiting schools

You may find that local schools would be interested in you visiting them to talk to students, to read to them or to work with them, say, on a book project or as part of a book sale/fair. Whilst some schools cannot pay you for such visits, others can, and you can learn the appropriate fee to charge by contacting any one of the authors' societies. This fee could also include expenses and you may find that some schools are able to remunerate you quite reasonably for a day or two's work. For some established authors, the fees from school visits make up a worthwhile percentage of their income.

Ask the headteacher if it is permissible for you to sell signed copies of your book to the students. Ask your editor or publicist if they can arrange for you to have copies and any promotional material, but make sure you give them plenty of notice. Check, too, that the students to whom you wish to sell your books are alerted to the fact that they should bring in some money on the day.

If you have arranged this visit yourself and it is a non-paying event, it may still be worth approaching your publisher to see if they are willing to pay some travelling expenses for you. They may also be able to provide you with promotional material, such as posters, postcards, badges, leaflets or bookmarks that feature your book, especially if it is part of a series which the publisher is promoting as a whole.

You may find that your publisher has produced a press release which they can give you, or perhaps a mail-order leaflet. Make your publisher aware that you are available and eager to do publicity work – this is likely to add impetus to any of the PR department's promotional ideas. If you are really keen and able to self-promote your work, then some research into publicity and marketing will help you with ideas. (Yes, there are yet more books available to guide you in this area.) Help your publisher to help you.

Tax and accounts

Whatever your circumstances, whether you are a taxpayer or not, or wherever you live, the tax situation for authors can get complicated. For a start, your income will fluctuate and cannot be accurately forecasted. Some bursaries are taxable, and so are some prize monies, to complicate your taxable income further. Various expenses, however, are deductible against assessable income for tax purposes if they are wholly and exclusively incurred in connection with your professional writing: these can include theatre and cinema visits for research purposes, and a proportion of your home expenses. Your local tax inspector or an accountant may be able to provide helpful advice. There are also media accountants who specialize in the vagaries of author taxation. If in doubt, seek expert advice. For now, keep every receipt and bill for purchases or services in connection with your writing.

What next?

And what of that next published project?

You *are* a new author. It is more than likely that your publisher will be waiting to see how the sales of your first work are going before committing themselves to publishing anything else by you. Before broadcasting your next work around the publishing community, check your contract. If you have a first refusal clause committing you to giving your present publisher your next book, it may include a timescale within which the publisher must come to a decision. If your publisher rejects your work, then the clause automatically fails and you are free to show your book to whomsoever you choose – as well as any subsequent work.

Chances are your editor will already have asked you what you are working on, or what you plan to work on next, or may even have made some suggestions as to where you might like to go from here. As long as you and your publisher have a good, stable working relationship, it makes sense for you to submit your work to them before showing it to anyone else. Your publisher will be just as anxious as you to build a lasting, profitable relationship, and it could take some years for an author's name to start registering with people.

Depending upon the type of market for which you are writing and the size of the publisher's list, you can hope that your publisher will buy from you between one and four new titles per year (providing, naturally, that your material continues to be suitable for them). On the other hand, you may be the sole author of a major series of which they wish to produce a new title every month. In that case, you are likely to be working flat out and to daunting deadlines. Always allow yourself enough time before agreeing to a delivery date, add in some extenuating circumstance time as well. Better to deliver early, than lose sleep because you have lost a week whilst your computer printer was being repaired.

If you are more prolific than your publisher can cope with, you may need to make some alternative arrangements. Could you branch out into fields which might interest different publishers? If you are able to broaden your scope by writing for different age groups or by writing on different subjects, then you will increase your marketability and you could find yourself working for several publishers at the same time without competing with yourself, and without upsetting your first publisher.

Self-publishing

Say you are absolutely convinced of the worth and value of a work that you have produced, yet the publishing world seems stubbornly blind to its merits. You are sure many people would enjoy your work if only they were given the chance to actually read it. What do you do when all the obvious options have been closed off?

Should you self-publish? First, ask yourself whether there really is a viable market for your book. A non-fiction title which covers a particular neglected subject, or which supplies an as yet undernourished need, is more likely to be successful than a typical novel or collection of poetry.

In other words, you should assess whether the rejection of several publishers has been on technical or economic grounds: that is, is it a good book for which they do not see a large enough potential market for them to gamble the money, or is everyone telling you that the book is poorly written or ill conceived? If the general assessment seems to be that there is something technically or stylistically 'wrong' with the book, then you should think very carefully before plunging into the world of self-publishing. Could it be that they are right and that you really need to spend some time polishing your skills? Consider this point carefully before committing time and money to a process that may result in you trying to find storage space for hundreds of unsold books starring Squish the Slug and his cheerful gang of invertebrate pals.

Let us suppose you do decide to go for self-publishing. Fortunately, with the existence of desktop publishing facilities and highly competitive printing prices, it is far easier now to publish yourself and less expensive than you might imagine. But do you have the time to learn the business? And do you have the necessary capital to cover the initial production costs? Self-publishing may not cost the earth, but it is a time-consuming business, as you need to absorb everything from how to get an International Standard Book Number (ISBN; you will find one on the back of every book published since the 1970s) to finding a distributor for the finished product.

Given the requisite time and money to set up the business, your next biggest headache will be figuring out how you are going to get your book in front of your potential customers in sufficient quantities to cover your costs. And we guess you would like to make a profit!

There are good books available on how to go about publishing your own work and, as with everything in this business, you will want to do some thorough research before you make a final decision. You will also discover the existence of small publishers (known as 'small presses') who may be able to help you publish and distribute your book if you can 'sponsor' them (that is, help out with the costs). It is helpful for publicity and distribution purposes if you can have your book on a publisher's list, no matter how small that publisher might be.

Before you publish a teaser sample of your work on your own or another website (or chapters or whole books online), ask yourself 'How am I going to make any money from this exercise, and is my work safe from theft and corruption?' Enough said!

Before you self-publish ask yourself the following questions:

- Why?
- Is there a real market for my book?
- Have I the time and resources to learn the business?
- Can I afford the expense and the risk of making a loss?
- Will I be able to sell the book to anyone other than my friends and family, who will expect free copies anyway?

Vanity publishing

A cautionary word on 'vanity publishing'. These people advertise regularly in magazines and newspapers, and you need to be careful about how you approach them. Vanity publishers always praise your work, no matter how unmarketable it really is. Vanity publishers are willing to publish *anything*, provided you come up with the money, but do you want your work published for the sheer vanity of it? Be very careful about your dealings with such operators and ask an author's society for advice or knowledge about any such company you may contact. At any given time, several vanity publishers will be under investigation for fraud. Better caution than burned fingers!

The bottom line

Now you have read through this book, does the life of a published author still look interesting to you? Even after everything we have warned you about? You are kidding? You *still* want to go ahead with it?

In that case, at least you are now armed with a lot more information than you were 12 chapters ago. The things we have written about here only scratch the surface of writing and publishing books. In many places we have recommended that you go and look out books that detail specific aspects of the business of writing and getting published. Remember that watchword is always *research*. The more research you do, the better your chance of hitting that elusive target.

Similarly, we hope we have given you a few pointers about how to go about collecting and organizing your ideas, producing a product which will attract a publisher and dealing with all the failures and successes that may accrue from your desire to see your name or your work in print. Over the years we have learnt the hard way, and made all the classic mistakes. We hope your learning process will be much faster than ours with the aid of this book.

In the end, it is all down to you. We can only provide the signposts: it is for you, as an individual author, to make the journey. And for that journey you will need persistence, determination, stamina, talent and a good deal of luck. Just keep one thing in mind: for an author, there is nothing more satisfying or fulfilling than to actually hold your first published book in your hands.

What are you waiting for? Publishers are crying out for new talent. Go and get that book published! Oh, and when you are rich and famous and living in tax exile, remember we had faith in you all that time ago when everyone else thought you would never make it.

Endnote

It took dozens of letters, faxes and e-mails, hours of phone calls, months of time and research and six drafts of the script to complete this book and deliver it to our very patient publisher, in between our normal day jobs, sleeping, eating, parenting and putting the cat out. We also used and abused friendships and family above and beyond the call of duty and are forever in their debt. One of the authors questioned added the following to the bottom of his returned questionnaire:

> *The question that really interests me is: how to write <u>my own</u> children's books – the satisfying and necessary ones – <u>and</u> to make contact with an audience. There are plenty of books and evening classes which only talk about market research and how-to-please-the-little-brats. (Don't write one of those, will you? I know you won't.)*

Sorry.

> *... but they all lived happily ever after.*

THE END

APPENDIX

Listings for UK-based authors

Books

Cassell's Directory of Publishing 2002, (27th edition, published annually) London: Continuum (in association with the Publishers Association), pp 520, ISBN: 0 826 45619 7, £75

Clark, Giles N. *Inside Book Publishing: A Career Builder's Guide* (3rd edition), (1994) London: Blueprint, pp 256, ISBN: 0 415 23006 3 £14.99 in paperback

The Ernst & Young UK Tax Guide for Authors, (1992) London: Ernst & Young, pp 68 [Out of Print]

Finch, *Peter How to Publish Yourself*, (1997) London: Allison & Busby Writers' Guides, pp 144, ISBN: 0 749 00301 4 £8.99

Krailing, Tessa *How to Write for Children (third edition)*, (1996) London: Allison & Busby Writers' Guides, pp120, ISBN: 0749 00258 1 £8.99

Legat, Michael *An Author's Guide to Literary Agents*, (1995) London: Robert Hale, pp 128, ISBN: 0 709 05572 2

Legat, *Michael Understanding Publishers' Contracts*, (1992) London: Robert Hale, pp 192, ISBN: 0 709 04638 3

L.M.P. (Literary Market Place) 2002 (pub Dec) – directory of the American Book Publishing Industry, R. R. Bowker, pp 2100 (two vols.), ISBN: 0 835 24393 1 £165

International LMP 2002 (directory of European publishers) pp 1400, ISBN 0 835 24430 X, £165 http://www.literarymarketplace.com – website of both, £250 for single user subscription

Quinton, Kathryn (ed.) *Book Trust Guide to Literary Prizes*, (1999) London: Book Trust, pp 48, ISBN: 0 853 53477 2

Turner, Barry *The Writer's Handbook 2002* (15th edition, published annually), London: Pan Macmillan, pp 800, ISBN: 0 333 90563 6 £12.99

Whitaker's *Books in Print 2000*, (published annually) Surrey: J Whitaker & Sons, (paper edition), 5 volumes, pp 13792, ISBN: 0 850 21280 4 (microfiche), ISSN: 0953-0401

Writers' & Artists' Yearbook 2002, (published annually) London: A & C Black, pp 699, ISBN: 0 713 65982 3 £12.99

Periodicals

The Author (in-house membership magazine of the Society of Authors, see below) Managing editor: Kate Pool (Deputy General Secretary), published four times a year, £7 per year.

Writing Magazine and *Writers News*
Writers News Ltd, PO Box 168, Yorkshire Post Newspapers Ltd, Wellington Street, Leeds, LS1 1RF. Tel: 01667 454441
Web: http://www.writersnews.co.uk Monthly, £43.90 per year.
Editor of both: Derek Hudson

The Bookseller
Published at Endeavour House, 189 Shaftesbury Avenue, London WC2H 8TJ. Subscriptions tel: 01795 414 500
Web: http://www.theBookseller.com
Weekly, £160 per year. Editor: Nicholas Clee

Books for Keeps (BfK)
6 Brightfield Road, Lee, London SE12 8QF. Tel: 020 8852 4953
Fax: 020 8318 7580 Editor: Rosemary Stones.

Carousel
The Saturn Centre, 54–76 Bissell Street, Birmingham B5 7HX.
Tel: 0121 622 7458 Fax: 0121 666 7526
Editors: Jenny and David Blanche. UK annual subscription: £9.75 for three issues in a year.

Children's Features
Cumberland House, Lissadel Street, Salford, Manchester M6 6DG

Publishing News
39 Store Street, London WC1E 7DS. Tel: 020 7692 2900
Fax: 020 7419 2111 Web: http://www.publishingnews.co.uk
Editor: Rodney Burbeck. £2 weekly, £99 per year.

Publishers Weekly
245 W. 17th St., New York, NT 10011, USA. Tel: 00 1 212 463 6758
Fax: 00 1 212 463 6631
Web: http://www.publishersweekly.com

Times Educational Supplement (TES)
Admiral House, 66-68 East Smithfield, London E1W 1BX.
Tel: 020 7782 3000 Fax: 020 7782 3200
e-mail: firstname.lastname@tes.co.uk Web: http://www.tes.co.uk
Editor: Bob Doe

Write to Publish
Author-Publisher Network, 12 Mercers, Hawkhurst, Kent, TN18 4LH.
Tel: 01580 753 346
e-mail: 100625.135@compuserve.com Web: www.author.co.uk
Published quarterly at £2.50, or £15 per year.

The New Writer
PO Box 60, Cranbrook, Kent, TN17 2ZR. Tel: 01580 212 626
Web: www.thenewwriter.com
Published 10 times a year at £3.50 or £32.50 per year.

World Wide Writers
Writers International Ltd, PO Cox 3229, Bournemouth, Dorset, BH1 1ZS.
Tel: 01202 716 043 e-mail: writintl@globalnet.co.uk
Web: www.worldwidewriters.com

Writers Forum
Writers International Ltd, PO Cox 3229, Bournemouth, Dorset, BH1 1ZS.
Tel: 01202 716 043 e-mail: writintl@globalnet.co.uk
Published six times a year at £3 or £18 per year. Two annual prizes for
poetry and short stories.

Contacts and Societies

Arvon Foundation:
- ■ Lumb Bank, Heptonstall, Hebden Bridge, West Yorkshire
  HX7 6DF. Tel: 01422 843714 Fax: 01422 843714
  e-mail: l-bank@arvonfoundation.org
- ■ Totleigh Barton, Sheepwash, Beaworthy, Devon EX21 5NS.
  Tel: 01409 231338 Fax: 01409 231144
  e-mail: t-barton@arvonfoundation.org
- ■ Moniack Mhor, Teavarran, Kiltarlity, Beauly, Invernessshire
  V4 7HT. Tel: 01463 741675 Fax: 01463 741733
  e-mail: m-mhor@arvonfoundation.org
  Web: http://www.arvonfoundation.org

Association of Illustrators (AOI): 81 Leanard Street, London
EC2A 4QS. Tel: 020 7613 4328 e-mail: penny.pearson@btinternet.com
Web: http://www.aoi.co.uk

Author's Licensing and Collection Society: Marlborough Court, 14–18
Holborn, London EC1N 2LE. Tel: 020 7395 0600 Fax: 020 7395 0660
e-mail: alcs@alcs.co.uk Web: http://alcs.co.uk

Book Trust: 45 East Hill, London SW18 2QZ. Tel: 020 8516 2977
Web: http://www.booktrust.org.uk

Children's Book Circle: c/o Puffin Books, 80 Strand, London
WC2R 0RL Tel 020 7010 3000 email: kerstin.grant@penguin.co.uk

Ernst & Young, Becket House, 1 Lambeth Palace Road, London
SE1 7EU Tel 020 7951 2000

Federation of Children's Book Groups: 2 Bridge Wood View, Horsforth,
Leeds, West Yorkshire LS18 5PE. Tel: 0113 258 8910
Fax: 0113 258 8920 e-mail: fcbg@cwcom.net
Web: http://www.fcbg.mcmail.com/fcbg.htm

International Board on Books for Young People [IBBY] (British
Section): c/o National Centre for Research in Children's Literature,
University of Surrey (Roehampton), Digby Stuart College, Roehampton
Lane, London SW15 5PH.
Tel: 020 8392 3008 Fax: 020 8392 3031
e-mail: ibby@roehampton.ac.uk Web: http://www.ibby.org

Public Lending Right: Richard House, Sorbonne Close, Stockton-on-
Tees, Teeside TS17 6DA. Tel: 01642 604699 Fax: 01642 615641
e-mail: enquiries@plr.uk.com Web: http://www.plr.uk.com

Publishers Training Centre: Book House, 45 East Hill, Wandsworth,
London SW18 2QZ. Tel: 020 8874 2718
Fax: 020 8870 8985 e-mail: publishing.training@bookhouse.co.uk
Web: http://www.train4publishing.co.uk.

Roger Palmer Ltd (Media, Contract and Copyright): Antonia House,
262 Holloway Road, London N7 6NE. Tel: 020 7609 4828
Fax: 020 7609 4878

Society of Authors: 84 Drayton Gardens, London SW10 9SB.
Tel: 020 7373 6642 Fax: 020 7373 5768
e-mail: authorsoc@writers.org.uk Web: http://www.writers.org.uk/society

Society of Young Publishers: c/o Endeavour House, 189 Shaftesbury
Avenue, London, WC2H 8TJ.
Web: http://www.thesyp.org.uk Chair: Karen Oldroyd.

The Writers' Advice Centre for Children's Books: Tel: 01737 242 999
Contact: Cherith Baldred.

Writers' Guild of Great Britain: 430 Edgware Road, London W2 1EH.
Tel: 020 7723 8074 Fax: 020 7706 2413
e-mail: postie@wggb.demon.co.uk Web: http://www.writers.org.uk/guild

Young Book Trust: 45 East Hill, London SW18 2QZ. Tel: 020 8516 2977
Web: http://www.booktrust.org.uk
And for children's books: http://www.booktrusted.com

National Association of Writers Groups: The Arts Centre, Washington,
Tyne and Wear, NE38 8AB. Tel: 0191 416 9751 *Link Magazine*

Irish Writers Union: Irish Writers' Centre, 19 Parnell Square, Dublin 1 Republic of Ireland. Tel: 353 (1) 872 1302 e-mail: iwc@iol.ie

Lancashire Authors' Association: 5 Quaker Fields, West Houghton, Bolton, Lancashire, BL5 2BJ. Tel: 01942 791 390 *The Record* – quarterly journal for members.

Federation of Worker Writers and Community Publishers: 67 The Boulevard, Tunstall, Stoke on Trent, Staffordshire, ST6 6BD. Tel: 01782 822 327 e-mail: fwwcp@cwcom.net Web: www.fwwcp.mcmail.com Quarterly magazine - £1.50 and broadsheet, 20p.

Websites:

http://www.booktrusted.com/handbook/prizes/prizesindex.html – List of prizes for writing for children.

http://www.bbc.co.uk/education/bookcase/ – BBC bookcase

http://www.libf.co.uk/page.cfm – the London International Bookfair

http://www.the-tls.co.uk – the Times Literary Supplement

http://www.cllc.org.uk – the Welsh Books Council

http://www.rslit.org/ – Royal Society for Literature

http://www.pen.org.uk/public/home.htm - PEN

http://www.bl.co.uk – The British Library

http://www.worldbookday.com – World Book Day

BIOGRAPHIES

Allan Frewin Jones

I was born. I deeply resent the fact that the cat stays at home whilst I have to go to school. I grow up. I deeply resent the fact that the cat stays at home while I have to go to work. I resolve to discover some way of avoiding going to work. I write 12 children's books in tea breaks, lunch hours and evenings. They're all rotten. I write children's book number 13. It is better. I re-write it 30-squillion times and it gets published. About 60 books follow. Most are published. Some in different languages. I stay home writing books. Ha! All I need to do now is find some way of getting that cat out to work.

Lesley Pollinger

I studied art, history of art, and literature and joined the police force. After eight years I left. I then planned to be an earth mother. Seven months after Crystal Rose, I joined the family firm. I acquired Bethany Jay and lots more children, including those belonging to other people. The agency suggested I was the right person to extend their children's author client list. I studied more art, literature, computer and publishing courses. Now I lecture on those courses, and write self-help books for my own and other people's teenagers. LIFE → THIS WAY? Yes, please!

INDEX